IMAGES
of America

Lost Stories of West Coast Latino Boxing

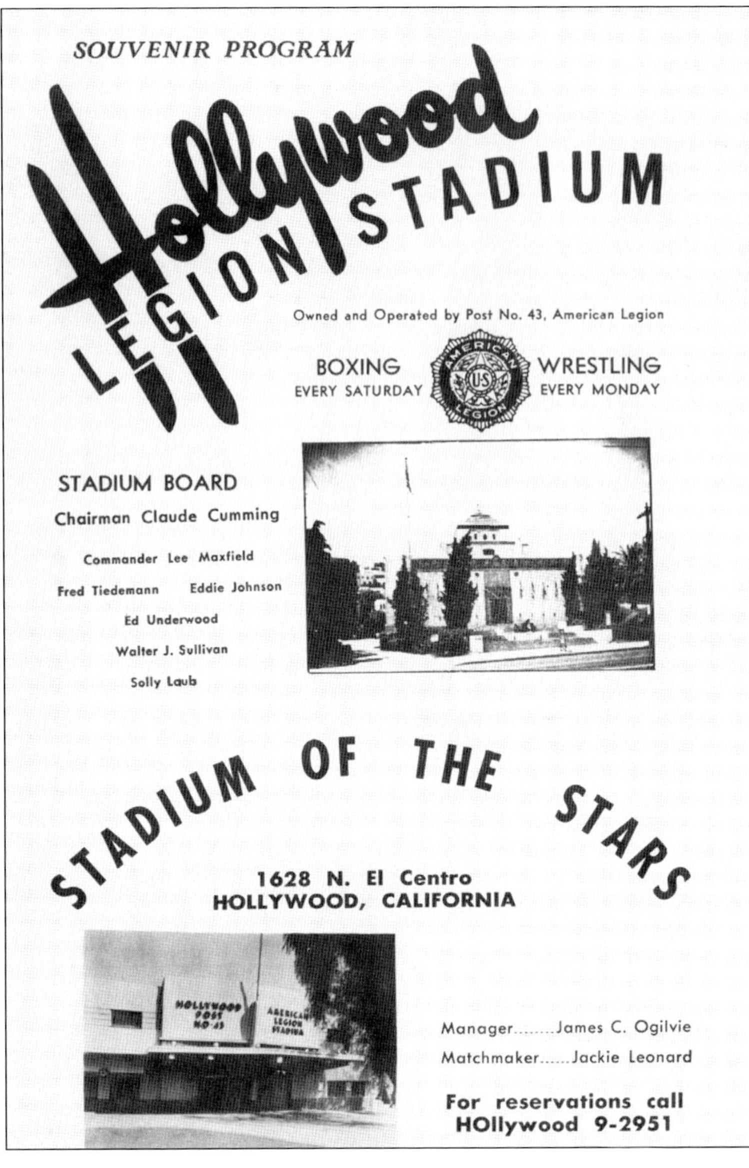

The Hollywood Legion Stadium, one of the major boxing venues on the West Coast, was known for its live musical programs and celebrity clientele such as Rudolph Valentino, Charlie Chaplin, Errol Flynn, Mae West, Humphrey Bogart, Clark Gable, the Marx Brothers, George Burns, Jack Benny, Bob Hope, Bing Crosby, George Raft, Frank Sinatra, and Dean Martin. Owned and operated by American Legion Post No. 43 since 1919, the "Legion" (capacity 6,300) enjoyed success with matchmakers Baron von Stumme, Cal Working, "Hap" Navarro, and Jackie Leonard until its last boxing show on September 12, 1959. It was later converted into a bowling alley. (Author's collection.)

On the Cover: Boyle Heights featherweight Adrian Arreola began boxing at the age of 15 at the Hollenbeck Youth Center along with his brothers Memo, Cipriano, Margarito, and Jose "Ugly." The renowned Arreola boxing family of the Eastside attended Roosevelt High School and became decorated amateurs, then professional boxers. Adrian is being lifted up by his brother Memo (left) and friend Jesse Ornelas (right) after his victory over former WBC bantamweight champion Lupe Pintor (TKO 8) in 1985; the fight was halted due to Pintor's left eye swelling shut. (Photograph by Carlos Baeza.)

IMAGES
of America

Lost Stories of West Coast Latino Boxing

Gene Aguilera
Foreword by Jimmy Lennon Jr.

ISBN 978-1-4671-0732-7

Published by Arcadia Publishing
Charleston, South Carolina

Printed in the United States of America

Library of Congress Control Number: 2021941794

For all general information, please contact Arcadia Publishing:
Telephone 843-853-2070
Fax 843-853-0044
E-mail sales@arcadiapublishing.com
For customer service and orders:
Toll-Free 1-888-313-2665

Visit us on the Internet at www.arcadiapublishing.com

This book is dedicated to the ones I love: Maria Aguilera, along with my daughters, Emily Aguilera and Melanie Aguilera. "You're my soul and my heart's inspiration." God has blessed me.

CONTENTS

Foreword

"If things get out of hand, just hide under the ring and you'll be safe."

The words uttered long ago by my father, Jimmy Lennon, remind me that along with the thrills and excitement of a great fight at the famed Olympic Auditorium in Los Angeles, there was often an element of danger and even the possibility of a riot. Undoubtedly, the legendary Latino boxers of the LA area have been incredibly exciting to watch as they inspired loyal and even rabid fans and created an atmosphere unrivaled elsewhere in the world.

Growing up the son of a world-famous boxing announcer, my sports heroes were mostly boxers . . . and primarily fighters with ties south of the border. I was enamored with the skills of Salvador Sanchez, the power of Lupe Pintor, and the charisma of Bobby Chacon. These warriors were veritable idols to many, as they were fighting not just for a payday but as representatives of their country, their community, and their devoted followers.

Like so many, I could literally feel the electricity and excitement in the air upon entering the Olympic on fight night. Smells of sweat and beer along with deafening sounds of cheers and boos reverberated throughout the cement walls. The anticipation of the main event intensified throughout the night and climaxed as the timekeeper struck the bell to start the fight. It's no wonder that the impassioned fans were brought to a nearly uncontrollable frenzy.

I actually never felt the need to follow my father's advice to take shelter under the ring, as I perceived I was recognized and respected by the crowd. Case in point—when Lupe Pintor defeated Jorge Lujan in a highly anticipated showdown in 1982, the crowd went wild, the celebration got out of hand, and a riot ensued. I vividly recall numerous fans halting their festival of fisticuffs to say hello to me and make sure I was OK.

I applaud Gene Aguilera for unveiling the rich accounts of these tremendous Latino warriors who have provided us fans with unforgettable memories.

—Jimmy Lennon Jr.
International Boxing Hall of Fame Ring Announcer

Acknowledgments

In pure affection to my family for surrounding me with their love: Maria "Chuyita" Aguilera, Emily Aguilera, Melanie Aguilera, Monica Felix, and our puppy, Prince. Thank you for living my dreams with me. In appreciation of the fine staff at Arcadia Publishing: Caroline Vickerson, Erin Vosgien, Chrissy Smith, Sara Miller, and Sarah Haynes. Gracias to the following boxers for your support: Ruben Olivares, Carlos Palomino, Armando Muniz, Danny Lopez, Alberto Davila, Frankie Duarte, Carlos Zarate, Alfonso Zamora, Oscar Muniz, Herman Montes, John Montes, Humberto "Chiquita" Gonzalez, Israel Vazquez, Rene Arredondo, Mike Anchondo, Greg Puente, Joey Orbillo, Willie Lucero, Louie Loy, and Dub Huntley. A special thank you to Danny O'Keefe for the honor of writing "El Corazon Mexicano" with you. High fives to the following photographers: Carlos Baeza, Theo Ehret, George Rodriguez, Linda Platt, Reed Hutchinson, Willie Romero, Rudy Mondragon, and Nate Wren. In appreciation to Jimmy Lennon Jr. for writing the foreword to my book—you are the direct link from the Olympic Auditorium until now. Thank you to Jim Berklas, Jim Berklas Jr., Steve DeBro (*18th & Grand*), Bill Dempsey Young and Linda Young (National Boxing Hall of Fame), John Echeveste and Abelardo de la Peña Jr. (La Plaza de Cultura y Artes), Rudy Tellez, David Martinez, Ned Doheny, Mark Guerrero, Dan Navarro, Raul Jaimes, Ernesto Amador ("No Puedes Jugar Boxeo"), Frank Aragon, Manuel Barba (Traffic Records), referee Joe Cortez, Fred Hermosillo (Boyle Heights/East LA Alumni), Humberto Terrones (radioespacio.org), Hector A. Gonzalez (Rampart Records), Melissa Alvarenga (USC Dornslife College of Letters, Arts, and Sciences), Richard Santillan, Anthony Gonzalez (Route 66 IECA Cucamonga Service Station), John J. Raspanti (maxboxing.com), Dennis Taylor (ringsideboxingshow.com), Roberto Diaz and Karla Ramos (Golden Boy Promotions), Craig Hamilton, Paul Thorne, Dan Hanley (cyberboxingzone.com), James DelCampo (heavybagboxing.com), Anson Wainwright (*Ring* magazine), Bill Caplan, Ray Mendoza, Joe Adame, Harvey Kubernik, Larry Battson (Wild World Talk Radio), Brian Young, Quincy Shelton (The Talk 2 Q Radio Show), John "Guapo" Maresca, Lee Groves, Mayor James Gomez, Juan Antonio Rios, Josh Kun, Brianne Davila, Brittany Davila, Ary Olivares, Oscar Zarate, Glenn Barnett, Jose J. Ramirez, John Wood, Dave Westgarth, Martha Najera ("La Reina del Boxeo"), and Alfred Godinez. Much gratitude to the *Los Angeles Times*, *Los Angeles Herald-Examiner*, *Sports Illustrated*, *Esto*, *Ring Mundial*, and all the libraries that graciously hosted our book presentations. In memory of Bob Recendez, Richard Orozco, Danny Valdez, and Jose Angel Barajas.

Unless otherwise noted, all images appear courtesy of the author.

INTRODUCTION

Boxing was our first sport, and will probably be our last. Humans are an easily provoked species. . . . But don't look away from boxing too soon. It comes too naturally to us, is too visceral, too much a part of human reflex. Boxing will die only when there is only one of us left. Even so, the last person standing will be found sparring in the moonlight, jabbing at shadows.

—Chris Erskine
Los Angeles Times columnist

Many West Coast Latino boxers have entered and departed the ring, their anecdotes left behind like another stain on the mat. Lost Latino boxing stories have floated around for ages without the benefit of being passed down from generation to generation. Buried tales and colorful narratives of beloved Mexican ring idols such as Ruben Olivares, Mando Ramos, Carlos Zarate, Danny "Little Red" Lopez, Bobby Chacon, Carlos Palomino, and Alberto Davila are showcased in these pages, their stories revived because no champion deserves to be forgotten. Other overlooked heroes and one-hit wonders of the golden era of Southland boxing (1940s–1970s) will also be saluted, along with the bygone contenders of the barrio who never saw their names in neon lights.

Singer/songwriter Danny O'Keefe pays homage to these ring warriors in "El Corazon Mexicano": "From the mean streets of Tepito/Torreon or Culiacan/With their hearts and their fists on fire/They burn brightly and they're gone./All of them enter the ring/To take or be taken apart/They all have one thing in common/They all have the Mexican heart."

Bill Dempsey Young of the National Boxing Hall of Fame (and son of acclaimed referee Dick Young) reminisced about the glory days: "A lot of that mystique is gone. It was just another level of macho back in the day. It's not as gritty as it used to be. There was a shady side of boxing and gangsters were very deeply involved. A lot of betting went down ringside at the Olympic Auditorium. Art Aragon could tell you a lot of those stories."

Poet and Beach Boys songwriter Stephen Kalinich writes of every boxer's dreams and fulfillment in "Be A Champion," "All of the strength rises within you. You are the future. You are the goal. This is the time to reach beyond limits to overcome weakness. To be in control. . . . In your heart you know, it is your time to win. And only one can win. Be a champion."

As I looked over old boxing programs and newspaper clippings, lost stories kept leaping off the pages. Now, some may view them as funny, sad, inspiring, or shocking—their inclusion here is not meant to glorify the mistakes of others but to allow people to learn from them. It has all happened so many times before—a talented boxer comes from a poor family, begins to make millions, then things go haywire.

Take this profession seriously or become a stepping stone for upcoming talent on the way up. WBC president Jose Sulaiman recalled the fate of a former Mexican ring sensation: "Ricardo 'Pajarito' Moreno left a lesson in life for current and future generations—that mountains of dollars and health are not eternal and that the major knockouts of boxers are received outside of the ring."

Boxing mirrors one of the basic tenets of life—you win some, you lose some. If you have ever witnessed a comeback in boxing, it is as exciting and exhilarating as any sports event, with an aura of unpredictability on full display and a story line laid out for the world to see. Anything is possible, and that is why I love the sport so much.

Let's touch gloves. May the best man win.

One

Forgotten Heroes and "One-Hit Wonders"

He died as we should all die: young, pretty, and a millionaire.

—Mexican sportswriter Pedro Morales describing
the unsung, colorful fighter Mauro Vazquez,
known as the "Tony Curtis of Tlaxcala"

This chapter is dedicated to the forgotten boxing heroes of yesteryear—the common man, the one-hit wonders of the ring who never saw their names in neon lights, boxers who had their day but shortly thereafter faded into the horizon, never to be heard from again.

Many boxers compiled a high number of losses on their ring record as they fought past their prime. They needed to provide a living for their families, and boxing was the only thing they knew how to do. Many thought the checks would never end.

These obscure ring warriors entertained at Southland punch palaces such as the Olympic Auditorium, Hollywood Legion Stadium, Ocean Park Arena, Vernon Arena, Gilmore Field, South Gate Arena, Wilmington Bowl, Eastside Arena, Valley Garden Arena, and El Monte Legion Stadium. They left a mark in their neighborhoods, became local celebrities, and basked in their 15 minutes of fame.

A local boxing scribe commented, "Fabulous days. A kid from the corner, born with God-given talent, could get some hype." Top Rank, Inc., boxing promoter Bob Arum explained to Lance Pugmire of the *Los Angeles Times*, "The sport is refreshingly like show business. Somebody comes from nowhere, gets a chance, becomes recognized, becomes a superstar. Great for the sport—a Cinderella story with some truth to it that gives a lot of hope to kids laboring in obscurity."

Some were heavy-handed hitters who never took a step back, and some ran all night, lucky to get out alive. In *Dreams of Ghosts that Roam the Olympic Auditorium*, manager Frank "kiki" Baltazar wrote, "Some fighters on this list were top-ranked fighters who fought for world titles and became champions, and some who fought for titles but never became champs, and some, because of the politics in boxing, never got a title shot. And some on the list never got out of the prelims but nevertheless fought their hearts out as their dreams of fighting at the famed arena became a reality."

Many boxing scholars regard Solly Smith (born Solomon Garcia Smith; 1871–1933) as the first world champion from Los Angeles and the first Mexican American to win a world title. Smith, whose father was Irish and mother was Mexican, held the world 118-pounds title (1896), world featherweight title (1897), Featherweight Championship of the Coast (1891), and Bantamweight Championship of Southern California (1891). Smith compiled a record of 29 wins (18 knockouts), 13 losses, and 20 draws while fighting from 1888 to 1904.

At many of Bert Colima's Southland fights, devotees of the masterful boxer filled the air with a familiar battle cry to cheer on their adored warrior. As explained in *Gentleman of the Ring: The Bert Colima Story*, "A few weeks later, on September 3, 1926, the movie stars were out to see their favorite, Bert Colima. Lupe Velez 'The Mexican Spitfire' started yelling, 'Geev eet to heem, Colima.' With that, Colima's legendary ringside chant was born."

Middleweight boxer Epifanio Romero, of Whittier, changed his name to Bert Colima to prevent his mother from knowing his profession. As stated in Colima's biography: "During these trying times [the Great Depression], boxing fans found a young Mexican American who gave them a reason to cheer, to forget about the world; even if it was only for a few rounds. . . . To his beloved fans, and to a Mexican American community who had few heroes upon which to place their hopes, he was their champion." On the days of Colima's fights at the Vernon Arena, outdoor family picnics blended with loyal fans waiting in line, creating a colorful and festive atmosphere. Sportswriter Jimmy Kilty noted, "The good looking Mexican did much for boxing, because it was the ambition of every Latin youngster to become another Colima. He was their idol. The great influx of Mexican boys that took up boxing paved the way for the revival of the sport in the Golden State." Pictured at the Main St. Gym in 1932 are, from left to right, Colima, Mexico national welterweight champion Alfredo Gaona, and "Mexican" Joe Rivers.

Larry Cisneros, nicknamed the "Rock of New Mexico" for his heavy body blows, was a popular Los Angeles lightweight contender managed by Gus Wilson. In two memorable bouts in 1943, during World War II, Cisneros was knocked out twice by future middleweight champion Marcel Cerdan of France before fellow GIs in Algeria. Cisneros, a Purple Heart–decorated veteran, ended his boxing career with a record of 72 wins (21 knockouts), 15 losses, and 5 draws while fighting from 1937 to 1948.

Famed two-time bantamweight world champion of the 1940s Manuel Ortiz was described by *Ring* magazine as a "notorious partier and playboy whose prime was shortened by his lifestyle." Ortiz (left), shown with referee Benny Whitman, made up for his short height with raging rights and left uppercuts. Ortiz was complimented by all-time boxing great Willie Pep, "Manny was the first man I ever sparred with; that experience alone should have been enough to make me hang up my gloves right then and there." (Photograph by Charles Heath.)

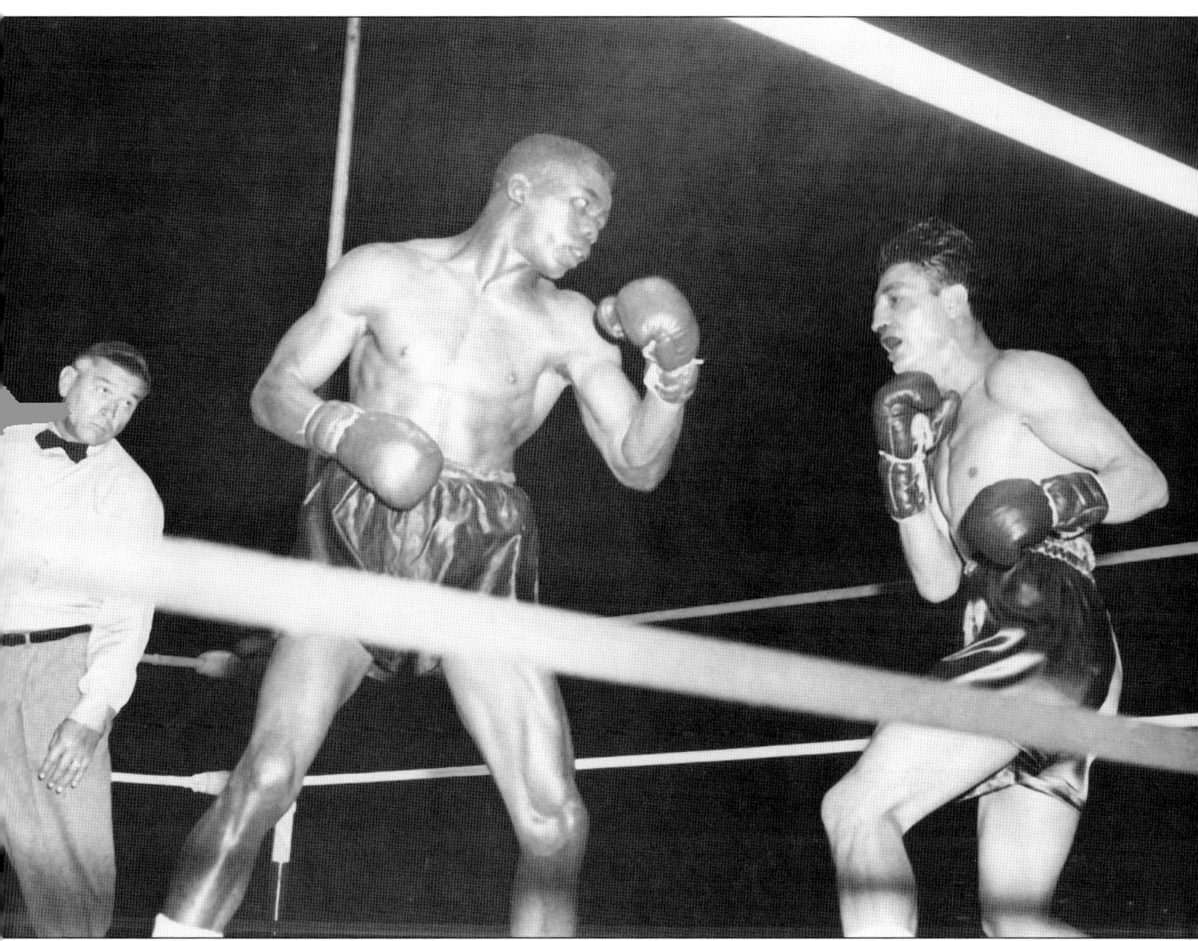

On May 25, 1948, world lightweight champion Ike Williams (center) eked out a hotly contested win (SD 15) over revered Los Angeles boxing idol Enrique Bolanos (right) at Wrigley Field as referee Charley Randolph looked on. George Main, of the *Los Angeles Herald-Express*, described the chaotic after-fight scenario in Williams's dressing room: "An officer, wearing a large badge on his plain suit, barred the entrance. Former featherweight champion Chalky Wright later admitted that Williams was in too much pain from Bolanos's left hooks to the body to be seen by anyone." Wright continued, "Williams had been half carried up the steps leading to his dressing room and once there collapsed on the rubbing table. He was unable to move, let alone sit up, and man, they didn't want anyone to know about it." The *Daily News* wrote, "The record crowd of 25,332 fans, with thousands turned away, poured a gross of $152,867.30 through the turnstiles for a new outdoor fistic record in Los Angeles." Williams was paid $48,000, while Bolanos took home $18,000 in the Cal Eaton–promoted event that was deemed too large for the Olympic Auditorium. (Courtesy of Hector A. Gonzalez.)

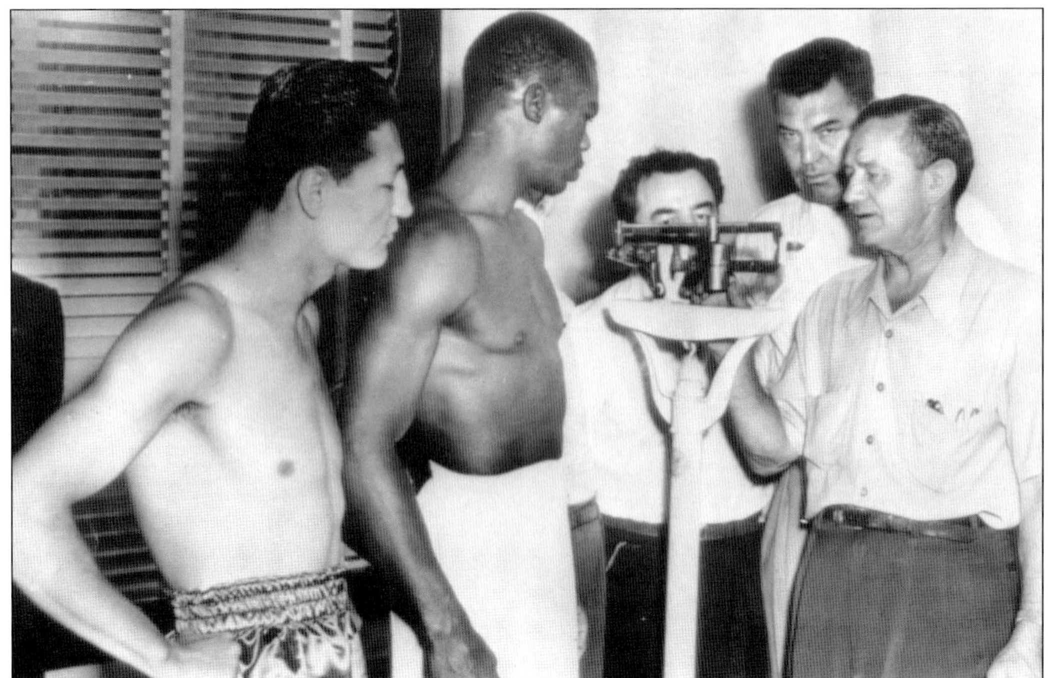

Pictured above are, from left to right, Enrique Bolanos, Ike Williams, Frank "Blinky" Palermo (Williams's manager), Jack Dempsey (referee/former heavyweight champion), and Willie Ritchie (chief inspector, California State Athletic Commission) at the weigh-in for the world's lightweight championship held on July 21, 1949, at Wrigley Field. In their third meeting before 19,000 fans, icy assassin champion Williams dropped the hawk-nosed Bolanos twice before the fight was halted (TKO 4), but Bolanos's manager, George Parnassus, claimed, "As early as round one, Bolanos insisted Williams was using his thumb" and "vowed to have an eye specialist prove this caused Bolanos's left eye to close." Williams, in his seventh title defense, simply claimed, "I was never better." Below, Chicano music pioneer Lalo Guerrero (left) and Bolanos (second from left) ring in New Year's Eve in 1951. (Below, courtesy of Mark Guerrero.)

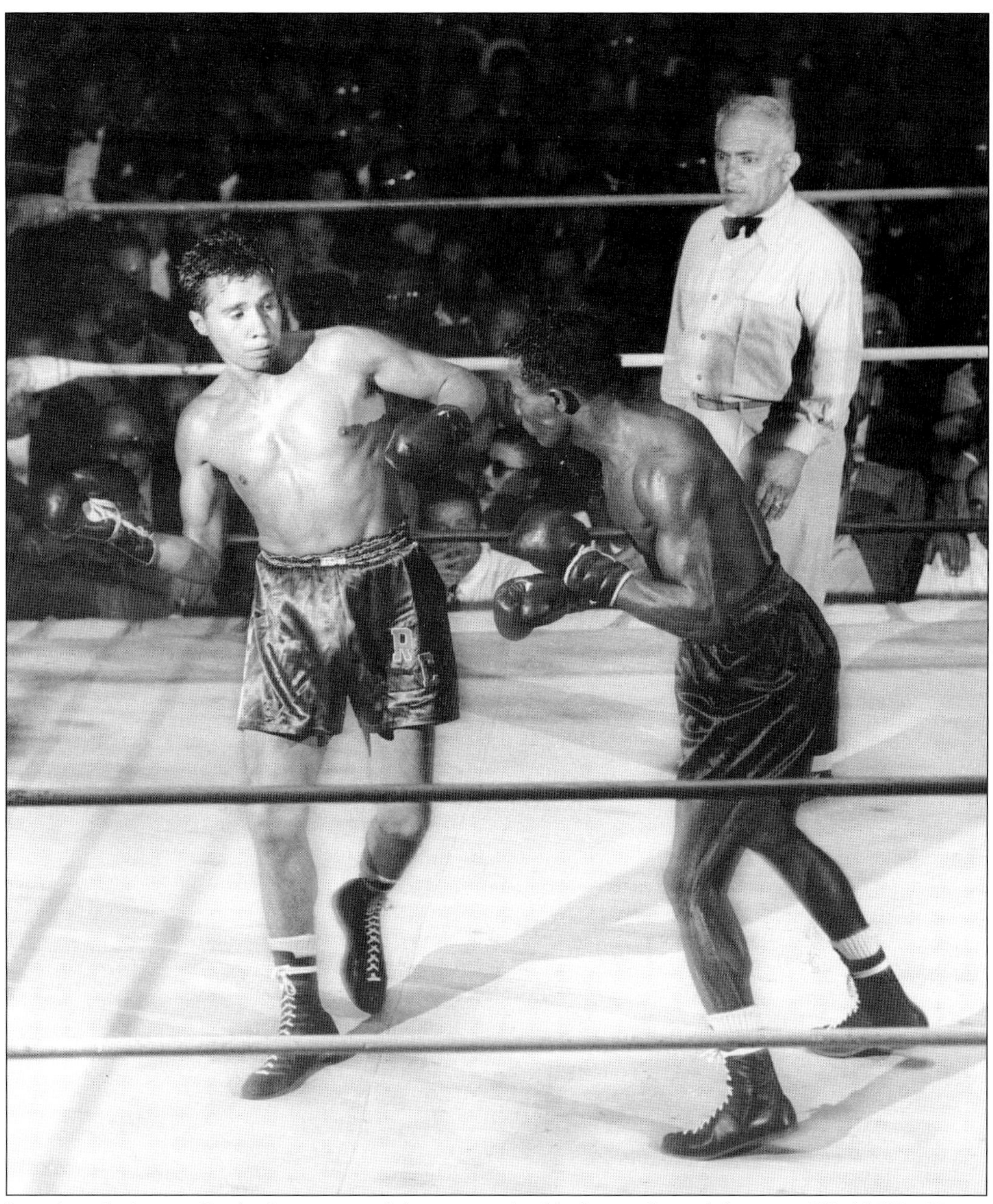

Los Angeles's own Rudy Cruz, one of the top-ranked lightweights of the post–World War II era, was awarded a Purple Heart for his Army infantryman duty in Europe. Promoter Don Fraser remembered Cruz as "a classy boxer who fought everybody. Cruz was in the shadows of Enrique Bolanos. Bolanos was a puncher, Rudy was not. If he fought Bolanos, it would have been a good matchup, but the managers were feuding." Though he never challenged for the world title, Cruz defeated future lightweight world champion Jimmy Carter (MD 10) on November 29, 1949. Managed by Gus Wilson, the clever but light-hitting Cruz (younger brother of middleweight boxer Costello Cruz) fought from 1943 to 1952, ending with 49 wins (11 knockouts), 10 losses, and 3 draws. In this image, Cruz (left) is fighting Tommy Campbell at the Olympic Auditorium on September 7, 1948, as referee Benny Whitman looks on.

Rudy Garcia, a two-time California featherweight champion, won the belt both times at the Hollywood Legion Stadium with victories over former world champion Harold Dade (TKO 11) in 1950 and Al Cruz (UD 12) in 1954. Called "Boxing's Two-Fisted Tamale," Garcia (right), of Los Angeles, is shown stopping Nate Brooks (TKO 4) in 1955. Managed by Lee Boren, the popular Garcia earned impressive wins over Lauro Salas and "Toluco" Lopez while fighting from 1948 to 1957. He ended his career with 35 wins (19 knockouts), 13 losses, and 1 draw.

After a decorated amateur career, crafty featherweight Al Cruz trained at the famed Main St. Gym in downtown Los Angeles. Called "a good local boy from Roosevelt High School and a good club fighter" by boxing fan Richard Orozco, Cruz compiled stirring victories over Rudy Garcia, Billy Peacock, and Chico Rosa but was outpointed by Filipino ace "Flash" Elorde in a tough 10-round loss in Manila. Cruz closed with 23 wins (8 knockouts), 6 losses, and 2 draws while fighting from 1950 to 1956.

Ramon Fuentes, one of the most interesting and colorful characters in Los Angeles boxing history, fought under the alias "Chuck Moody," moonlighted as a gravedigger, and eventually developed into a solid contender along with his younger brother Jesse, a middleweight. After winning the California welterweight championship in 1952, the rugged and busy Fuentes (second from right in the above image) successfully defended his title six times. Fuentes (at right in the below image) beat the best of his era, including Art Aragon, Billy Graham, Kid Gavilan (at left in the below image), Mario Trigo, Charley Salas, Joe Miceli, and Chico Vejar. Promoter Don Fraser stated, "Fuentes wasn't popular because of his style. He was not an entertaining fighter. Just a straight-ahead type of fighter, like Gene Fullmer—a bull-style guy." Fuentes fought from 1950 to 1958, ending with a record of 41 wins (12 knockouts), 16 losses, and 1 draw.

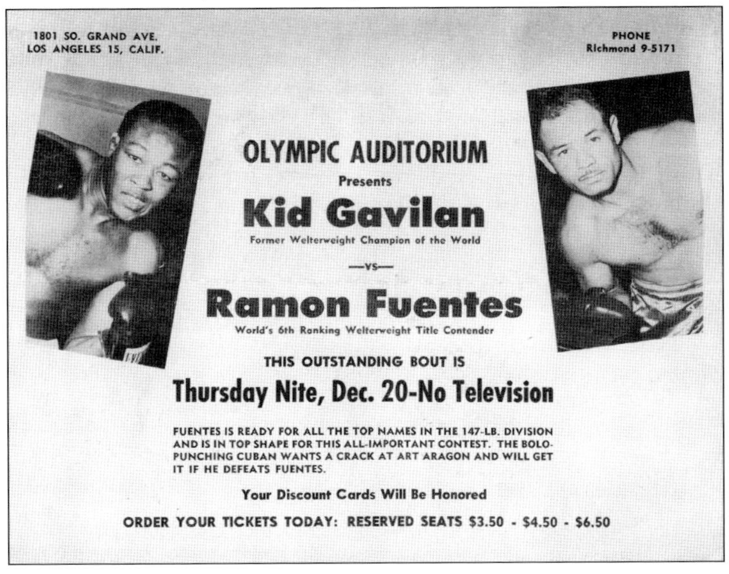

Matchmaker Gabriel "Hap" Navarro (left), pictured with sports editor Rudy Garcia of *La Opinion*, was born a few blocks from the Olympic Auditorium. His son, singer/songwriter Dan Navarro, recalled, "My dad lived and breathed boxing. It was his first love." Hap, nicknamed after 1900s cartoon character Happy Hooligan, was an encyclopedic resource of Los Angeles boxing. At 17, Hap began sports writing for *La Opinion*; next, he became publicity director at Hollywood Legion Stadium (featuring the column "The Latin Touch"); then, he was promoted to assistant matchmaker (a job he held from 1948 to 1953) under Baron von Stumme and Cal Working. After finally reaching the coveted matchmaker job (and serving in that role from 1953 to 1955), Navarro was abruptly forced out of the Legion under mysterious circumstances. His sudden departure has always been a matter of conjecture in Los Angeles boxing circles. "Things were getting dicey. Forces put pressure on him," Dan reflected. "They [the local underworld] basically said, 'Book my fighter.' Dad said, 'I get some guy handing me a $100 bill. I gave it back to him.' My dad refused any type of money payout. It seemed they wanted to put their own guy in there, so they put in Jackie Leonard."

Dan Navarro, son of matchmaker Gabriel "Hap" Navarro, continued: "The 1940s and 1950s were not a particularly positive time for Latinos in Anglo businesses, especially those as intense as boxing. Hap was a non-veteran, a Mexican American working at a stadium owned by the American Legion. That was a big factor." Publicist Don Fraser recalled, "Hap didn't come up the typical rank and file. There was a lot of hostility against him. A lot of backstabbing and personal jealousy. Hap got tired of it and quit in 1955." Dan concluded, "With the pressures of the constant barrage, dad, in fact, owned a pistol he was carrying, a World War II Beretta. My opinion why he's got the gun is, 'I've been threatened. I'm going to protect myself', and I think over time, that built up to where my mom said, 'Hap, you've got to get out of this completely. This is not how we want to live,' and my dad would have listened to that. It just got too rough and he moved us [his wife, Josephine, and three children] to Calexico. Though he loved his later life, he resented leaving the business." Pictured here are, from left to right, (seated) Hap and Josephine Navarro; (standing) *Los Angeles Times* writer John Hall and Rudy Garcia. (Courtesy of Dan Navarro.)

Willie Lucero, born and raised in West Los Angeles, attended University High School and was California state ranked in the featherweight division. A fan favorite at the Olympic Auditorium, Ocean Park Arena, and Hollywood Legion Stadium, Lucero's top purse in the ring was $345, which made a full-time job at Douglas Aircraft (and later Woodland Furniture) a necessity in order for him to support a family of five. Lucero's son, Ruben, recalled, "My dad had a fight scheduled, and with less than two weeks to go, his opponent backed out. So, he went off of training and celebrated with wine, women, and song. With a few days' notice, Babe McCoy (Olympic Auditorium matchmaker) called and said he had to keep the date. My dad said no and got blackballed. Afterward, Babe was indicted for fixing fights, and my dad got to fight again, but was past his prime and became an opponent." Lucero, known as a "rugged little gamester," retired with a ring record of 16 wins (7 knockouts), 9 losses, and 3 draws, collected while he was fighting from 1954 to 1961. (Courtesy of Ruben Lucero.)

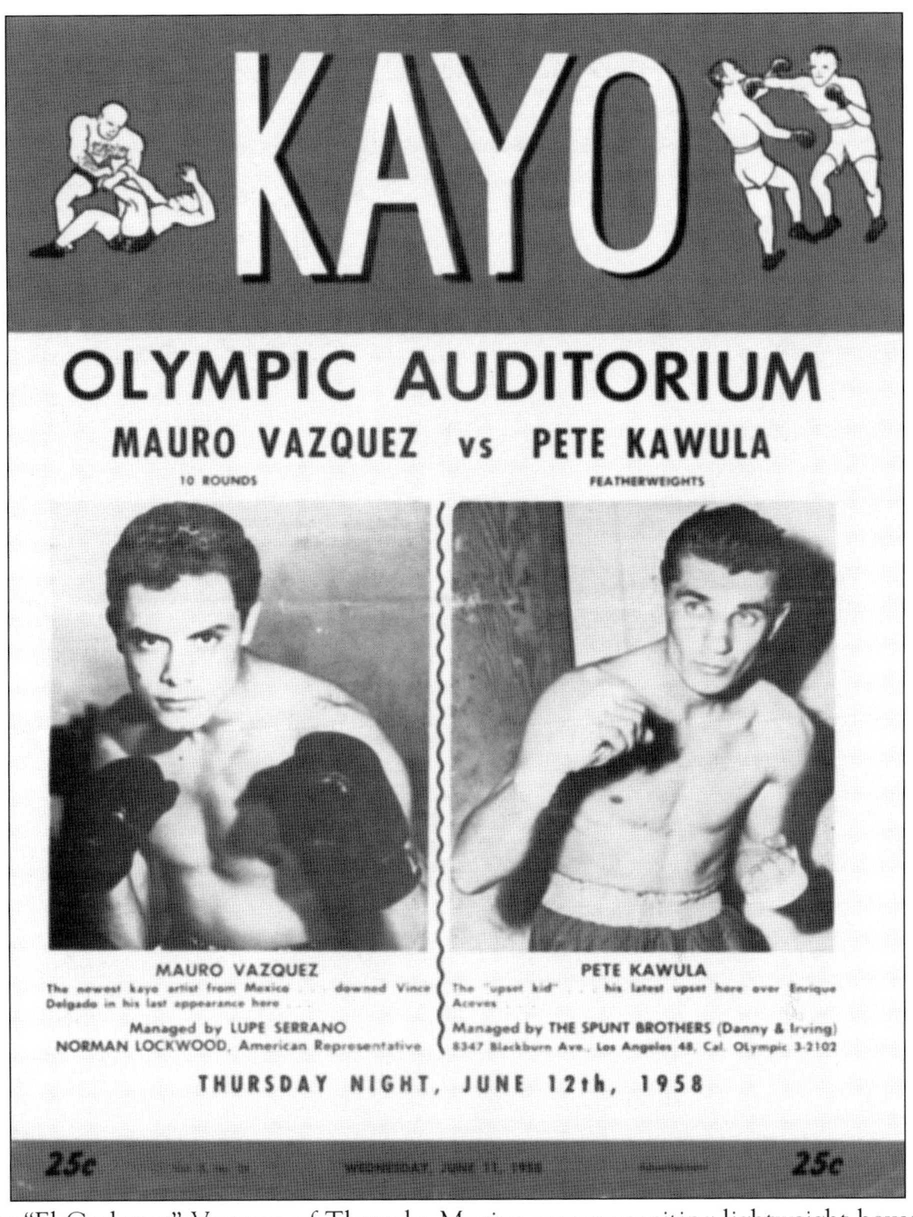

Mauro "El Cachorro" Vazquez, of Tlaxcala, Mexico, was an exciting lightweight boxer who delighted crowds from Mexico City to the Olympic Auditorium. With significant victories over Ike Chestnut, Cisco Andrade, Gil Cadilli, and Vince Delgado increasing Vazquez's popularity, the press began calling him the "Tony Curtis of Tlaxcala" due to his resemblance to the American film actor. Vazquez's blazing start (25–0) also earned him a spot on the cover of *Ring* magazine in 1959 as one of boxing's "Fast Rising Attractions." Sportswriter Pedro Morales wrote of Vazquez, "He awoke in his fights a rare reaction in boxing, when fans become horrified to see a young man with the face of a movie star, bleeding, sometimes his face slaughtered, wasting his courage towards a public that did not know how to deal with that kind of situation." An educated, well-dressed ladies' man, Vazquez had a colorful résumé that included stints as an amateur bullfighter, furniture business entrepreneur, and mayor of Xaltocan (in his home state). Vazquez ended his career with 35 wins (27 knockouts), 11 losses, and 1 draw while boxing from 1957 to 1965.

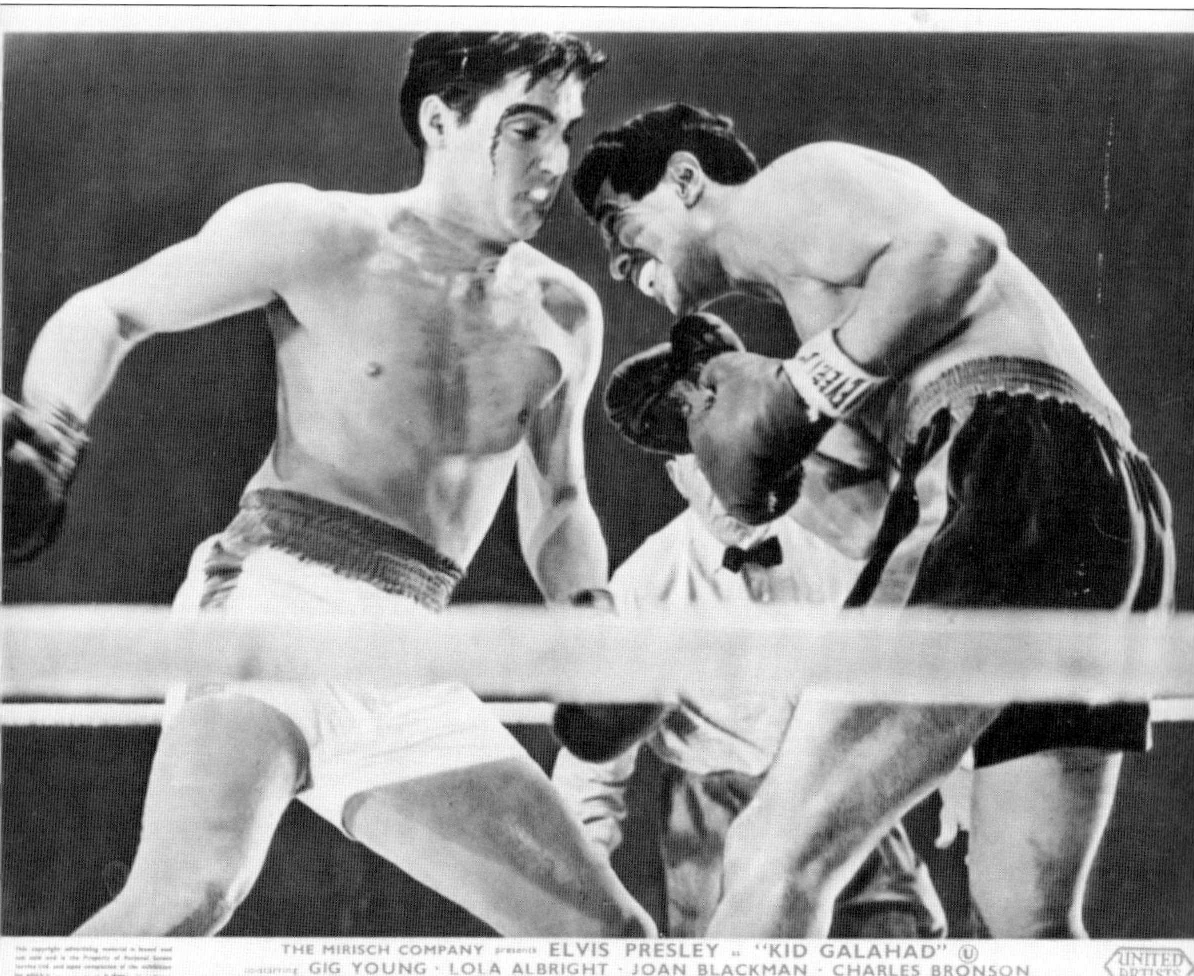

Middleweight Orlando De La Fuente (birth name Roy), from the Seventh Street neighborhood in downtown Los Angeles, was managed and trained by his father, Bob, along with his younger brother Ralph as chief second. At the beginning of Roy's career, he was not of age, so his father used another son's (Orlando) identification to qualify Roy for a boxing license. Roy's oldest brother, Ray (boxing as Ray Fuentes), remembered, "That's the way my dad would do things. He was like a little hustler. He was a character, big time." Ray, who attended Cathedral High School, recalled appearing in a 1962 film: "Throughout my boxing career, my father was a boxing consultant for the movie industry. While a consultant, he got me a role as a prizefighter [Ramon "Sugarboy" Romero] in a movie called *Kid Galahad* which starred Elvis Presley." Orlando, also appearing in *Kid Galahad* as a trainer/sparring partner for Presley, retired with 17 wins (3 knockouts), 9 losses, and 1 draw from 1961 to 1973. Ray (at right, fighting against Presley) closed his brief welterweight career with a record of 2 wins, 0 losses, and 1 draw while fighting from 1955 to 1958.

Two

Mexican Ring Idols Invade Sunny California

Down there in the 1950s, I watched fighters named Memo Diez, Joe Medel, Joe Becerra and Pajarito Moreno, most of them bantamweights, well-taught fighters who were true to the valiant Mexican tradition of accepting pain as part of life's portion.

—From "Macho Palace," an article about Mexico City's Arena Coliseo by novelist/journalist Pete Hamill in the *Los Angeles Times* magazine

The 1970s became a time for a mass invasion by a revered and talented group of boxers from Mexico who graced the shores of sunny California. As *Boxing Illustrated* stated, "[They] came to Los Angeles, as sooner or later do all good Mexican boxers." Boxing columnist Bill O'Neill described their value to Southern California: "Mexican boxers and those who idolize them have long been the very lifeblood of our area."

Veteran boxing publicist Bill Caplan described Efren "Alacran" Torres's disputed 1964 split-decision loss to Japan's Hiroyuki Ebihara that caused a frightening and costly riot at the Olympic Auditorium: "There were more police and firefighters than I'd ever seen. It proved the dedication of the Mexican fight fans to their heroes. If they think their man gets the short end, they'll let the world know about it."

In one of the greatest fights in Los Angeles history, two elite warriors, Carlos Zarate and Alfonso Zamora, lined up against each other at the Forum on April 23, 1977. The program read, "Boxing promotions at The Forum are more than prizefights; they are expressions of nationalism. Thousands of fans motor up from south of the border. They arrive in aged cars or crowded pick-up trucks. Some come from as far away as the Yucatan Peninsula. They clutch tickets purchased from agents in border towns such as Tijuana and Mexicali."

Olympic Auditorium matchmaker Don Chargin explained the excitement of pitting a good local fighter against a good Mexican fighter and watching the lines of fans stretch around the block to get in: "We used to get as many as 10,000 tickets down to Mexico. They'd drive across the border, show their fight tickets and get a 72-hour pass. Nobody needed to show a passport."

After winning the world title in 1959, baby-faced slugger Jose Becerra was hailed as the next great Mexican bantamweight king. But in a homecoming tune-up bout on October 24, 1959, at Arena Coliseo in Guadalajara, Jalisco, Mexico, Becerra delivered a heavy-handed knockout (TKO 9) over Walt Ingram, a 24-year-old club fighter from Weirton, West Virginia. Becerra helped Ingram to his stool, where minutes later, he collapsed; Ingram died 29 hours later at Mexican American Hospital from brain-related injuries suffered in the fight. In this image, manager Pancho Rosales (third from left) and Becerra (second from right) carry Ingram's flag-draped coffin. Within less than a year, Becerra was shockingly knocked out in eight rounds by journeyman Eloy Sanchez in a nontitle fight on August 30, 1960, in Juarez, Chihuahua, Mexico. With no aggressiveness or passion left for the sport, Becerra, the reigning world bantamweight champion, retired from boxing at the age of 24. Two years later, on October 13, 1962, in his hometown of Guadalajara, Becerra announced a special one-off comeback fight to benefit a local injured fighter named Rudy Coronado. After winning a six-round decision over veteran Alberto Martinez, the religious Becerra graciously donated his purse to Coronado.

The boxing career of Cuban-born Ultiminio "Sugar" Ramos (above, center) was roiled in controversy and tragedy. On November 8, 1958, in Havana, in his 12th professional bout, Ramos felled fellow countryman Jose Blanco in the 8th round. Sadly, Blanco succumbed from injuries endured in the contest. Five years later, in 1963, Ramos knocked out WBC/WBA featherweight titleholder Davey Moore in the 10th round at Dodger Stadium to become world champion; unfortunately, Moore passed away a few days later from brain damage suffered in the fight. The fatal match would provoke iconic singer/songwriter Bob Dylan to pen the song "Who Killed Davey Moore?" In addition, Los Angeles Dodgers president Walter O'Malley proclaimed that boxing would no longer be welcome at his family-oriented stadium. Shown below are, from left to right, Ramos, Luis Rodriguez, Roberto Cruz, Raymundo "Battling" Torres, Moore, and Emile Griffith.

Sugar Ramos (right) is shown during his intense battle with WBC/WBA lightweight champion Carlos Ortiz at El Toreo de Cuatro Caminos, Mexico City, on October 22, 1966. After Ramos suffered a bad cut on his left eyelid in the second round, referee and former champion Billy Conn halted the fight in the fifth stanza (chosen as "Round of the Year" by *Ring* magazine) and awarded the victory to Ortiz of Puerto Rico. Conn's decision to stop the contest was based on the advice of Dr. Gilberto Bolanos Cacho, but the doctor later admitted there might have been a language miscommunication. Conn remained bitter afterward: "The fact that Ramos had to have 28 stitches vindicated my decision. I put much of the blame on the doctor's shoulders. If he had stood with me, the trouble would have been avoided. But then he became shaky; he was terrified and got out of the ring. He should have stayed there. He was known to the crowd. I was a stranger. He didn't have the guts to back up his opinion."

Angry with referee Billy Conn's decision to stop the fight, the pro–"Sugar" Ramos Mexico City bullring crowd of 35,000 began to riot. Puerto Rican–born lightweight champion Carlos Ortiz is shown being pelted with coins, stones, and bottles as he exits the ring. The *Beaver County Times* printed this about one of boxing's most bizarre moments: "[Twenty] minutes after Ortiz had returned to his dressing room, [WBC vice president] Ramon Velazquez ordered him to return to the ring and continue the fight. When he refused, Velazquez declared Ramos the winner and new champion." Velazquez, sitting at ringside, overruled Conn's decision and accused the referee of favoring and allowing Ortiz to use dirty tactics. The *St. Petersburg Times* reported that Velazquez said Conn "took 13 seconds in the second round [after Ramos dropped Ortiz] to complete the mandatory eight-count." Two days after the fight, WBC president Luis Spota reversed Velazquez's call, declared the title vacant, and ordered a rematch due to the controversial stoppage. Noting the terrific pressure Velazquez was under, Spota said, "Velazquez's decision to declare Ramos the new champion was an emergency solution on his personal authority to calm the crowd."

Boxing Illustrated's Jack Welsh spoke of Cuban exile Jose "Mantequilla" Napoles and Mexican ring idol Ruben Olivares: "These two superstars from Mexico City were virtually twins in their flamboyant lifestyles and they were equally explosive in the ring. [Forum promoter George] Parnassus said Napoles and Olivares complimented each other financially with exciting box office returns." Parnassus (left) and Napoles are pictured in the image at left. Sportswriter Tomas Benitez recalled, "Napoles was smart. He was beautiful. He was like watching Willie Mays play center field." The charismatic Olivares, in his prime, electrified the Los Angeles fight crowd, yielding throngs of flag-bearing, sombrero-waving, excitable fans packed to the rafters at the sold-out "Fabulous Forum." Below, Olivares (center) is shown with Televisa announcer Antonio Andere (left) and referee John Thomas.

Nightclub showgirls Diane Lewis (second from left) and Joni Carson keep bantamweight contenders Jesus "Chucho" Pimentel (left) and Jose Medel apart before their "Mexican Civil War" at the Los Angeles Sports Arena on December 6, 1965. The victorious Medel (UD 10) recalled the seesaw battle: "It was a solid right, a beautiful punch. I didn't hear the referee count one, two, or three. The first thing I heard him say was four." Pimentel said to *Sports Illustrated*, "When I got up, I could see nothing but blurriness. I remember picturing Medel like a bull in the ring, smoke coming out of his nose and kicking dirt, ready to charge." Pictured below are, from left to right, Rudy Clay (younger brother of Cassius Clay), Jose Luis Pimentel (older twin brother of Jesus), Jesus, and Cassius Clay (Muhammad Ali). (Below, courtesy of Victor Pimentel.)

The *Los Angeles Times* wrote, "Ruben Olivares came out of Mexico City with a destructive punch, a baby face, a carefree spirit, and a sharp, witty manner that endeared him to everyone. . . . Life has always been one great laugh for Olivares. He gets serious only in the ring. He still plays just as hard as he fights and is the bane of Mexico City writers who berate him for not leading an exemplary life to set an example for youth." Olivares said, "Boxing is hard work, and when a fight is over, it's time to have some fun. I'm seriously thinking of living in the United States. The writers in Mexico follow me around and will not allow me a private life. Here they realize a man is entitled to relax and enjoy himself between fights." Author/historian Bert Sugar described Olivares by saying, "Look at his number of knockouts. He was a dual champion. He was never in an unexciting fight. He had a left hook from hell. Everything about him said great fighter." (Courtesy of *Ring Mundial*, August 1968.)

Ruben Olivares (at center in the above image) told Anson Wainwright of *Ring* magazine, "Jesus 'Chucho' Pimentel [at left in the above image, with referee George Latka at right] was one tough hombre. We fought for my bantamweight titles at the Forum in 1971, but I was able to stop him in the 11th round. Pimentel put up with a lot of punishment. Interestingly enough, this was his one and only title fight, and he retires from the ring that night. I loved promoter George Parnassus [at left in the image at right] like a father, he believed in me, and tried to motivate me by offering to buy me a brand-new Camaro if I knocked Pimentel out by the fifth-round. I did try for the KO, but did not get it. Parnassus paid me $90,000 for the Pimentel fight, so I was able to buy a new car anyway."

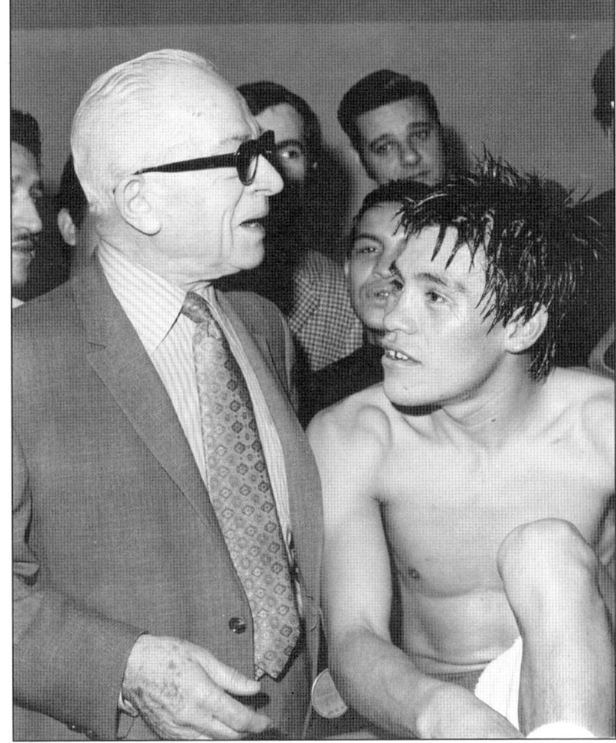

Ruben Olivares recalled his fight against top featherweight contender Art Hafey at the Plaza de Toros Monumental in Monterrey, Nuevo Leon, on March 4, 1973: "I underestimated Hafey at the time and thought it would be an easy win in Mexico." Hafey, the "Toy Tiger" of Nova Scotia, Canada, chimed in, "I don't think Olivares had much respect for me." Olivares continued, "I remember seeing Hafey at the hotel lobby early one morning. Just as he's getting ready to go running, I'm getting back in from an all-nighter. What an irony that was. . . . He was tough and threw a thundering right hand. Well, in the fifth round, Hafey put me to sleep, a deep sleep." Leo Noonan, of the *Los Angeles Herald-Examiner*, wrote of the Olivares-Hafey rematch at the Forum in 1974: "It is a pitch for Hafey's almost hermit-like style against the philosophy of playboy Olivares." Olivares (left), shown hanging onto Hafey, concluded, "I came in good condition to the rematch. I had to overcome a knockdown, but this time, I won a split decision."

Los Angeles Herald-Examiner sportswriter Allan Malamud wrote of the November 23, 1974, clash at the Forum between Mexico's Ruben Olivares and Alexis Arguello (attempting to become the first Nicaraguan to win a world title): "Olivares's World Boxing Association featherweight title will be at stake, and so will the pride of an entire nation. Arguello is the national idol as Nicaragua rebuilds [from the earthquake of December 1972] and tries to forget. Two hundred of his fans already are headed north in an automobile caravan. They will be joined in Inglewood by 800 more who had the money to pay for an airplane flight." Jack Hawn of the *Los Angeles Times* reported, "Olivares had been in command and seemed headed for an easy victory when the sharp-punching Arguello unloaded." Olivares (seated) recalled, "In the Arguello fight, I got caught with an uppercut in the 13th round and went down. When referee Dick Young [at left] got to four, he asked me, 'Ruben, do you want to continue?' I answered, yes . . . but not until next week."

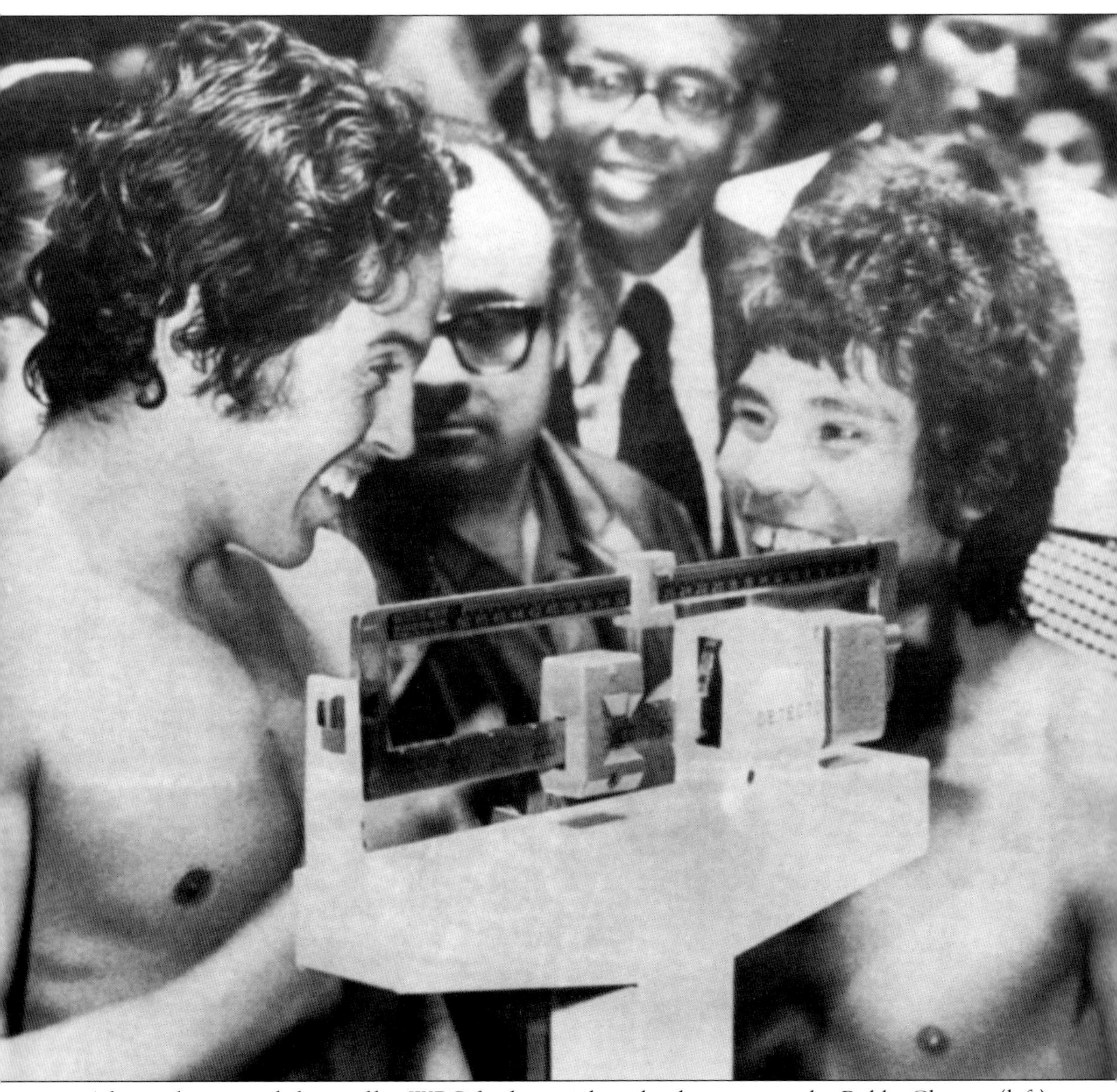

After making one defense of his WBC featherweight title, the ever-popular Bobby Chacon (left) prepared to meet his old nemesis, Ruben "Mr. Knockout" Olivares (right), on June 20, 1975. However, there was one major problem—there had been too many "in-between fight celebrations" for Chacon. John Hall, of the *Los Angeles Times*, wrote that Chacon was paid "$165,000 for his next one at the Forum, where the steam room and Ruben Olivares took it all away." Sportswriter Jack Hawn reported, "[Chacon] was knocked out in the second round, but a strong wind might've blown him over just as easily." Chacon recalled, "He didn't knock me out. I fainted." Olivares remembered: "After the fight, I quickly changed and went to the bar. I was dying of thirst. I asked the bartender for a beer, but he said they were sold out. Turns out we set the Forum record for beer sales that night. That's quite the honor."

Ruben Olivares was "nicknamed 'Rockabye Ruben' for his ability to put his opponents to sleep," said *Ring* magazine, "[his] weapon of choice was the deadly left hook. Don Fraser's main drawing card was Ruben Olivares, a bantamweight. He was to become the greatest moneymaker in the city's history, topping [Art] Aragon in that regard and rivaling [Enrique] Bolanos in the fanatic loyalty of his fans." Olivares reminisced, "Los Angeles means so much to me because I won all my four world titles at the Forum. I fought there 22 times. I don't think any other boxer is near that number. The Forum was like my second home. My home away from home. My representative, Gene Aguilera, told me the Forum has a plaque on the wall for Neil Diamond, celebrating his sold-out shows. He can't believe the Forum doesn't have one there for me. I fought there so many times, I know all the words to the National Anthem." Shown at the Forum in 1986 are, from left to right, cutman Phil Silver, Olivares, and cornerman Aguilera.

Se levantó de la lona en el primer round y...

OLIVARES KOT EN 2 A RAMIREZ

CD. OBREGON, Son., 28 de abril.— Rubén Olivares se repuso de una caída en el primer episodio y noqueó sorprendentemente al inicio del segundo round al zurdo sinaloense José Luis Ramírez, quien alcanzó a incorporarse después de caer por un zurdazo al mentón, pero sus "segundos" intervinieron porque estaba en malas condiciones y ahí se decretó el KOT. La pelea tuvo lugar esta noche en el Gimnasio Municipal, que registró una entrada de aproximadamente 5 mil espectadores.

Ramírez derribó al "Púas" en los albores del combate y después que el capitalino recibió de pie la cuenta de protección, procedió a acosarlo con golpes de todos los calibres. Olivares recurrió a veces a desesperados amarres y en algunos momentos trató de ripostar con disparos por dentro, y terminó el round casi al borde del nocaut.

El zurdo de Sinaloa se lanzó nuevamente al ataque al comenzar el segundo giro pero cuando más engolosinado estaba fue prendido por un gancho izquierdo que el explotó en el mero botón para desplomarse pesadamente en la lona. Ramírez se levantó cuando el réferi contaba seis segundos pero lo hizo tambaleante y en pésimas condiciones, por lo que sus "segundos" no dudaron en pedirle al tercer hombre que detuviera las acciones.

Antes, Rodolfo Chávez ganó decisión en 10 a Bernardo Ibarra (Información: El Imparcial de Cd. Obregón).

ACAPULCO.— El gallo local Fabián Palma noqueó con un oper de izquierda a la barbilla al tapatío Salvador Estrada. "Yuyo" Suástegui KOT en 2 al "emergente" Antonio "Chamaco" Hernández, y Miguel Bracamontes ganó decisión en 8 a Domingo Mayoral (Santos Obregón).

GUADALAJARA.— El pluma tapatío Rosendo Ramírez ofreció una magnífica exhibición de boxeo y venció por puntos en 10 rounds al leonés Pedro Martínez. En otra, Pancho Acosta KO en 5 al "Chino" Uribe. (Luis TOPETE).

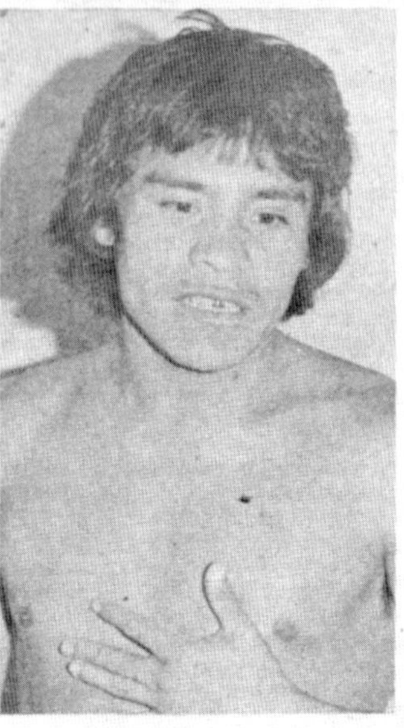

Rubén OLIVARES. Parecía que sería arrollado, cuando...

In the twilight of his career, former four-time world champion Ruben Olivares was offered up as a stepping-stone to 19-year-old southpaw Jose Luis Ramirez at Municipal Gymnasium, Ciudad Obregon, Sonora, Mexico. It was expected that Olivares would serve as a "name opponent," adding luster to the résumé of the popular upstart Ramirez (43–1). Olivares recalled the April 28, 1978, bout: "It was a tough fight because he was younger and he drops me in the first round, but I got saved by the bell. Back in my corner, I tell my manager, Pancho Rosales, 'Clean my gloves, put a lot of vaseline on my face, we're going to war!' In the second round, I catch him in the corner, feint a left hook to the body, and land a perfect left hook to the jaw. It was a thud heard across the arena. He was out cold . . . knocked out while standing up. The audience goes dead silent, and down he goes. His manager, Ramon 'Zurdo' Felix, comes rushing in, waving the white towel, but it was too late. I knew he wouldn't get up. The referee could have counted to 100." (Courtesy of *Esto*.)

Ruben Olivares recalled, "The way [Jose Luis] Ramirez went down, I was, in fact, worried if he would ever fight again. But as we all know, Ramirez went on to be a world champion, and an impressive one at that. There were 5,000 fans in attendance, but to this day, I have never seen a video of that fight. It is a fight that has gone underground, under the radar. Like they don't want anyone to see it. But I know it was televised because I saw all the cameras." Significantly, in 111 total bouts for Ramirez, boxing royalty such as Alexis Arguello, Ray "Boom Boom" Mancini, Edwin Rosario, Hector "Macho" Camacho, Pernell Whitaker, and Julio Cesar Chavez were unable to stop him before the final bell. Olivares concludes, "Many years later, I run into Ramirez at a boxing event, and he introduces me, 'Son, I want you to meet my other papa. This is Ruben Olivares. The only man ever to knock me out.'"

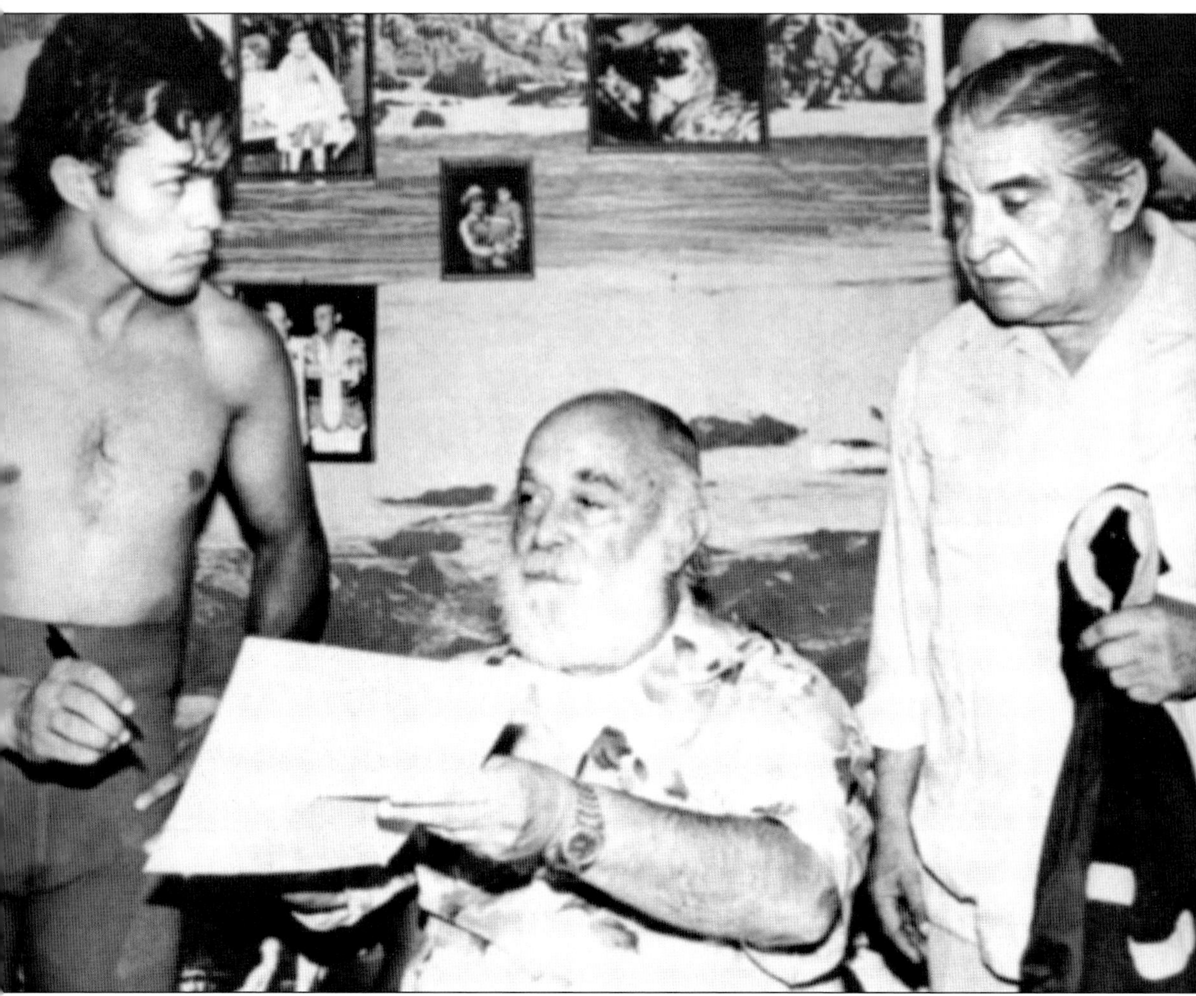

Jack Hawn of the *Los Angeles Times* wrote of 19-year-old WBA welterweight champion Jose "Pipino" Cuevas, "The image is all wrong. A shy, gentle face, wavy, neatly-groomed hair, deeply serious, religious, non-smoker, non-drinker, family-oriented, enjoys camping and outdoor activities, owns six meat markets, two apartment buildings and seven other lots in and around Mexico City, trains diligently." Matchmaker/adviser Rafael Mendoza said this of the stone-faced assassin Cuevas: "His condition is excellent. He runs early in the morning, has breakfast at 8, goes to the gym at 12, eats his big meal at 4, and relaxes. That's it. He's never been a playboy." Hawn described a typical Cuevas fight night: "'May-hee-co! May-hee-co!' It's a familiar chant in Southland arenas—sometimes a roar that threatens to shatter eardrums and boil blood. The scene also is familiar. Spurred by the crowd, the Mexican fighter reaches back for a second effort, starts hammering his non-Mexican opponent relentlessly, and finally knocks him out in a crescendo of near insanity." Cuevas (left) looks to manager Lupe Sanchez (right) for guidance as he gets ready to sign a contract with promoter Harry Kabakoff.

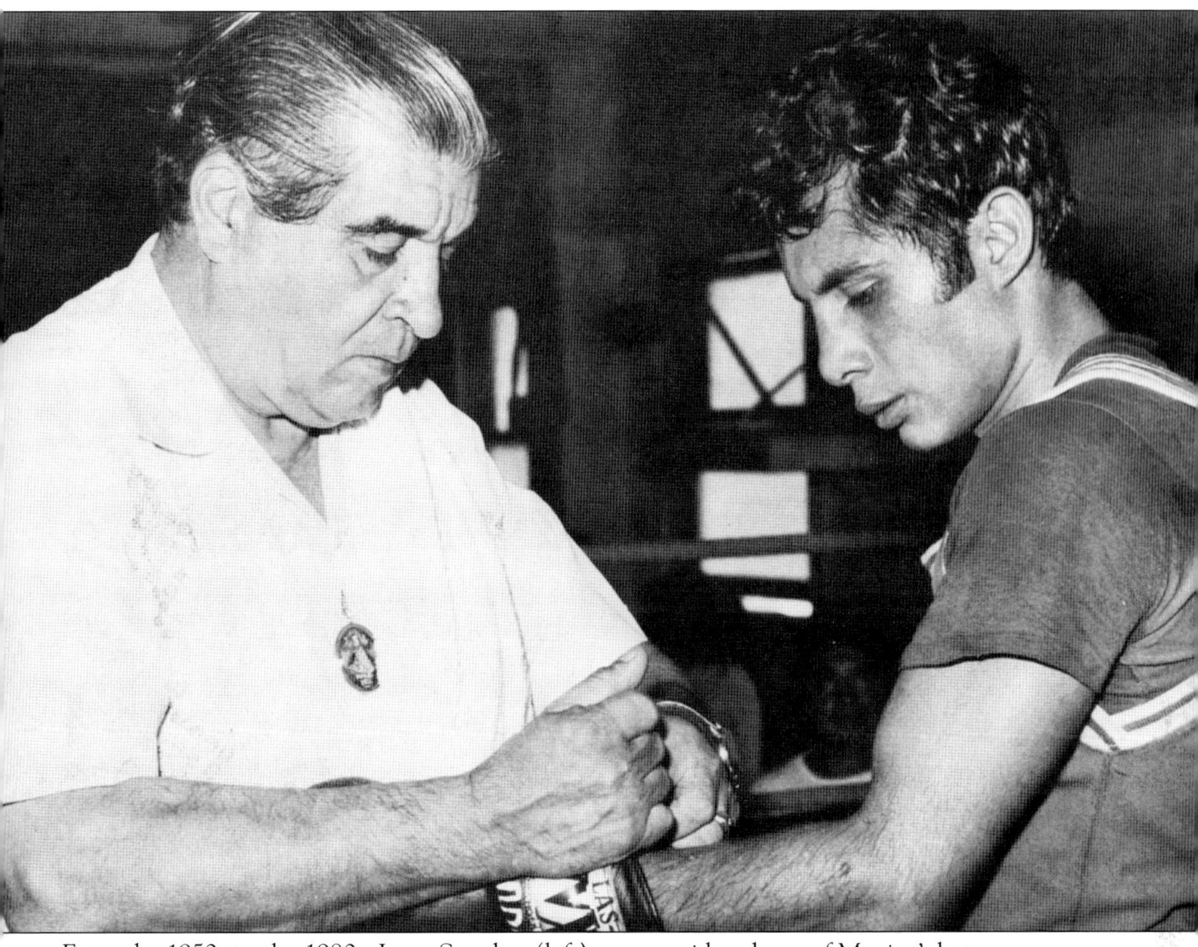

From the 1950s to the 1980s, Lupe Sanchez (left) was considered one of Mexico's best managers, along with Arturo "Cuyo" Hernandez and Pancho Rosales. Assisted by longtime trainer Justo "La Manzana" Sanchez, Lupe worked diligently out of Gimnasio Margarita in Mexico City with a rotating stable that included Ricardo "Pajarito" Moreno, Jose Medel, Marcos Geraldo, Rodolfo "Gato" Gonzalez, Marcos Villasana, and Humberto "Chiquita" Gonzalez. Lupe Sanchez's first world champion was bantamweight Rodolfo Martinez (right), in 1974, followed by welterweight titleholder "Pipino" Cuevas in 1976. Steven Losch, writing in *Experience the Golden Age of Boxing*, observed, "Sanchez exercised absolute control over Pipino's life, in and out of the ring, forcing him to lead a monastic existence." Cuevas remembered Sanchez's strict demeanor: "Lupe always came in and turned off the air-conditioner in our rooms. It didn't matter if it was hot outside. He was afraid we'd get sick." After Detroit's Tommy "The Hit Man" Hearns memorably dropped Cuevas face-down in the second round of their title bout on August 2, 1980, Sanchez jumped in and stopped it, saying, "A dozen world titles aren't worth the life of a fighter."

John J. Raspanti of maxboxing.com described welterweight contender (and former shrimp-boat fisherman) Zovek Barajas: "Tall and rangy, Barajas, when serious, was dangerous. A couple of years before, he had upset ranking contender Armando Muniz and former welterweight champion Billy Backus." Born Hipolito Barajas, he was professionally known as Zovek, with his first name inspired by travelling Mexican magician and escape artist Zovek the Great. The curly-haired ladies' man (of Escuinapa, Sinaloa, Mexico) fought from 1971 to 1984, ending his career with 22 wins (19 knockouts), 14 losses, and 1 draw. Above, Jimmy Lennon (right), ring announcer at the Olympic Auditorium since 1943, interviews Barajas (center) and Spanish publicist Luis Magana in 1975. In the image at left, wrestler Andre the Giant (center) holds boxers Barajas (top), Frankie Duarte (left), and Danny "Little Red" Lopez (right) like toy dolls. (Both photographs by Theo Ehret.)

Up-and-coming welterweight Carlos Palomino (left) and rugged, crowd-pleasing Zovek Barajas tussled for 10 hard rounds at the Olympic Auditorium on February 13, 1975. *Los Angeles Herald-Examiner* sports editor Bud Furillo wrote of Barajas, "He has everything; poise, pride, and the look and instincts of a predator." In the final round of the toe-to-toe slugfest, Barajas dropped Palomino to one knee, but Palomino quickly recovered to his feet for a close majority draw. In the rematch, held six weeks later at the Olympic, Palomino's new game plan of not backing up resulted in a nine-round, action-packed TKO victory over the switch-hitting Barajas. Promoter Aileen Eaton heaped praise on boxing sensation Palomino: "A classic fighter learns it almost by instinct. Some can never learn because they have a different style. Take Carlos Palomino. Jackie McCoy, a great trainer, works with him. Carlos used to go in and brawl. He waited for the punch. Jackie taught him to avoid punches, how to box. He's really a good fighter now because he moves forward, jabs, hits."

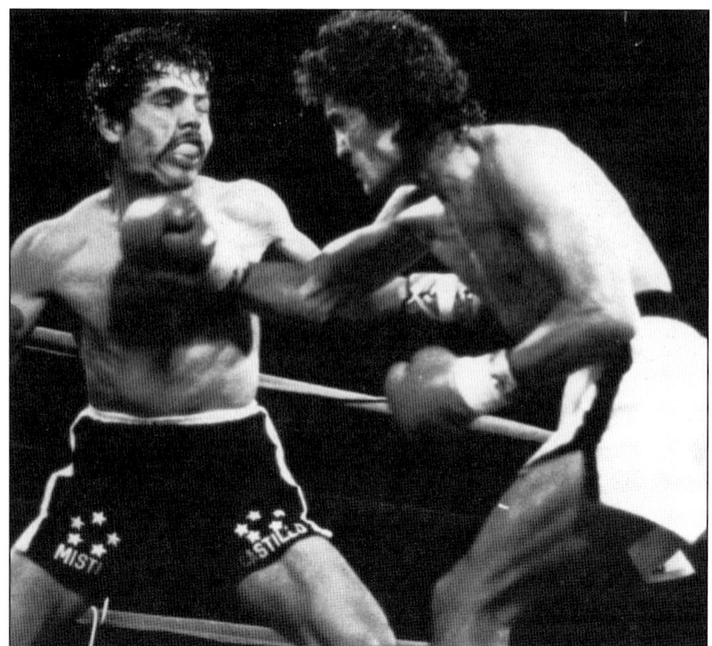

Howard Cosell, of ABC's *Wide World of Sports*, said of WBC featherweight champion Salvador Sanchez (right): "His first defense was against Ruben Castillo, from Bakersfield, California, in Tucson, Arizona, April 12, 1980. Castillo fought cleverly, even brilliantly built up a lead. But then in the late rounds, it was all Sanchez, as he won the decision." An upset Castillo disagreed with the judges' scoring (UD 15), telling *Sports Illustrated*, "Why should I feel bad? I won the fight. The way it looked today was I had to knock him out to get a draw."

Ring magazine's Don Stradley wrote of the Salvador Sanchez (left) vs. Wilfredo Gomez (right, with promoter Don King in the center) clash at Caesars Palace, Las Vegas, in 1981: "Jose Torres [former light heavyweight champion] said at the time that Americans were probably shocked by the rowdiness of the crowd, but were finally seeing 'our national Latino disposition.' King took notes. So did Bob Arum. The bout, won by Sanchez on an eighth-round KO, rammed home the idea that Mexicans and Puerto Ricans were a combustible combination." (Courtesy of *Alarma!*)

Rene Arredondo of Apatzingan, Michoacan, Mexico, was the first Mexican-born boxer to win a world title in the super lightweight division. Arredondo, a two-time world champion, was managed by Ricardo Maldonado while being trained by his older brother Ricardo Arredondo and Ernesto Gallardo. The tall and lanky Rene Arredondo, nicknamed "Caña Brava" ("Brave Sugarcane"), won the WBC super lightweight belt from champion "Lightning" Lonnie Smith of Denver, Colorado (TKO 5), on May 5, 1986, at the Olympic Auditorium. Rene won his second world title when he defeated champion Tsuyoshi Hamada (TKO 6) in a rematch held at Kokugikan, Tokyo, Japan, on July 22, 1987. Rene, a popular mainstay at the Olympic Auditorium in Los Angeles, also picked up the California super lightweight (1983) and WBO NABO super welterweight (1995) titles. Arredondo, shown at the Main St. Gym, fought from 1979 to 1997, ending his career with a record of 46 wins (40 knockouts) and 12 losses. (Courtesy of Rene Arredondo.)

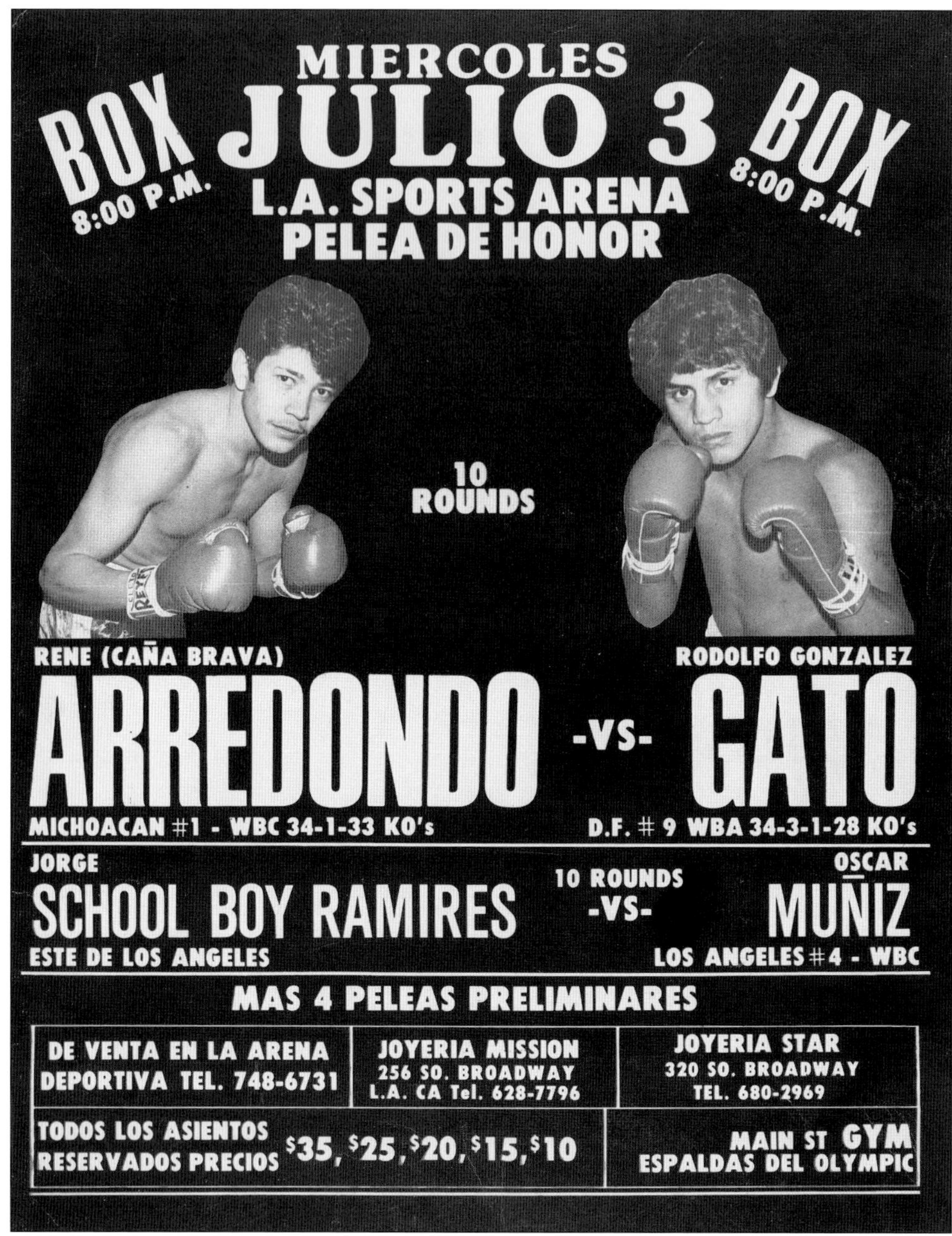

In the aptly titled "Fight for Honor," super lightweight Rodolfo "Gato" Gonzalez of Mexico City defeated fellow countryman Rene Arredondo in a 10-round split decision at the Los Angeles Sports Arena on July 3, 1985. Arredondo, dropped in the first round by a Gonzalez right cross, recalled, "This was the toughest fight of my career. I was hit a lot. Many called it 'Fight of the Year.'" Boxing sportscaster Fernando Paramo told *Hoy* newspaper, "When the fight was over, Rene Arredondo's hands were basically broken. You could not see Gato Gonzalez's face. When the doctor arrived, he attended to both fighters. Both of them were totally submerged in ice. Both of them with faces massacred." Sadly, Gonzalez was convicted of beating two neighbors to death during a drunken brawl at his home in Mexico City on October 5, 2007, and sentenced to 42 years in prison for the double homicide.

Three

Leaders of the New Breed

Boxing's new breed is a class breed. Fading fast from the scene is the concept of the unshaven, snarling fighter with the grimy clothes, grimier fingernails and the vocabulary of a Bessarabian baboon. Mostly, this concept was something out of Hollywood. But Hollywood drew its original illustration from real life. It was just that Hollywood never bothered to update the picture.

—*World Boxing* magazine, August 1969

An article in *International Boxing* magazine stated, "Mando Ramos is the exciting leader of boxing's new breed. He wears mod clothes and his hair is long. He doesn't wear a beard because officials do not allow fighters into the ring with beards, and besides, Mando may be too young to grow a beard. . . . But his mind was on other things, too—things with slender legs, long, dark hair and fluttering eyelashes. The 'Mod Kid' had captured the hearts of hardbitten California fight fans, and he's even attracted the teeny bopper set."

As a newly crowned champion, Ramos was introduced to the crowd at the Olympic Auditorium and appeared very dapper in his new hip suit and shiny shoes. The era of the late 1960s and 1970s ushered in a contemporary group of flashy and urban boxers, coined the "Youthquake" movement by *KO* magazine's Jeff Walton. According to an article in *World Boxing*, "[Ramos] epitomizes the youth that isn't satisfied today to take what is left over. . . . Hollywood, television—all the media. Wake up! Change the picture. Today's breed of fighter is new—new and refreshing."

This chapter also includes a cast of characters that was essential to the success of the Olympic Auditorium. After the fights, the "in" place to visit was the Carioca Family Restaurant (located at 2321 East First Street in East Los Angeles) for fine Mexican food and cocktails. Owner Margaret Torres ran the restaurant with an iron fist, while her son Jo Jo Torres (Forum Boxing training director) invited legendary fighters such as Ruben Olivares, Rafael Herrera, Jose "Mantequilla" Napoles, Lauro Salas, and Enrique Bolanos to his mother's establishment.

Olympic Auditorium matriarch and promoter Aileen Eaton was described by *Sports Illustrated* as such: "Dictatorial yet feminine, she is loved by some, hated by others, and feared by all." Eaton (standing) entered into an agreement with KTLA-TV Channel 5 to televise boxing every Thursday night at the Olympic, beginning on May 20, 1965, with Dick Enberg (center) and matchmaker Mickey Davies (right) calling the action. Enberg and Davies were succeeded by announcers Tom Harmon, Keith Jackson, and Jerry Coleman. In 1968, KCOP-TV Channel 13 began broadcasting boxing with Jim Healy at the microphone, followed by Tom Kelly and Stu Nahan. The top-rated weekly sports show *Boxing from the Olympic* was shown live in Los Angeles and Mexico and beamed (via delayed feed) into 35 cities across the country. Enberg's three-and-a-half-year stint announcing at the Olympic was his entry into the world of network sports broadcasting. Enberg, then 30, said of the tough, overbearing Eaton: "She had me in tears more than once. Always yelling in my earplug to read a promo or build-up an upcoming fight or something. She was some lady." WBA featherweight champion Raul Rojas of San Pedro is shown in the inset on the magazine cover.

Promoter Don Fraser (left) of Blythe, California, is shown with Gene Aguilera at the Forum during the late 1970s. Fraser, a graduate of Manual Arts High School, first worked as sports copy boy for the *Los Angeles Times*, then as editor of *Knockout* magazine (and scribe of "Van O Grams") before going to *Ring* magazine with his column "In Sunny California." The *Los Angeles Times* wrote, "In the promotional art of that era, nothing was too over-the-top for Don Fraser. There were strippers and boa constrictors and once a lion. Fraser promoted a lightweight named Lauro Salas, the 'Lion of Monterrey.' Fraser wanted to pose Salas with the real cat. He contacted a lion tamer and a zoo. 'This lion tamer brings out a ferocious-looking lion, who starts sniffing around all of us,' Fraser said. 'Salas, wearing boxing gloves, is instructed to stick his left arm into the lion's face, acting as if he were throwing a jab. The lion takes one look, opens his mouth and tries to take a bite out of Salas's arm. The only thing that saved him was his reflexes.'"

Jackie McCoy managed five world champions during his 55 years in boxing: Don Jordan (1958–1960), Raul Rojas (1968), Mando Ramos (1969–1970, 1972), Rodolfo Gonzalez (1972–1974), and Carlos Palomino (1976–1979). Born Warren Spaw (he changed his name to prevent his mother from knowing his occupation), featherweight McCoy logged a ring record of 34 wins (9 knockouts), 12 losses, and 5 draws from 1942 to 1951. Mando Ramos spoke of the "West Coast Wizard" to the *Los Angeles Times*: "I idolize the guy. If my son ever wanted to box, Jackie would be his trainer. That's what I think of him." Rich Roberts of the *Times* stated, "In a sport that certainly has its seamy side, McCoy has managed to walk through a mudslinging contest in a white tuxedo without collecting a spot." Sportswriter John Hall added, "They just don't make them like Jack anymore." Super bantamweight Georgie Garcia, managed by McCoy at the Westminster Boxing Club in Orange County, recalled, "Jackie was the best. I miss his Johnny Carson style. He was cool like that." From left to right are McCoy, Rojas, Ramos, and Palomino.

Jackie McCoy spoke to the *Los Angeles Times* about Mando Ramos: "I let him start to work out and knew at once that this baby-faced kid was something special. He had tremendous natural ability. There's no telling how great Mando could've been. I've never, ever seen a guy with the natural ability he had as a young man." Unable to box professionally as a minor in California, Ramos arranged to have his birth certificate altered, allowing him to fight three days after his 17th birthday, all unbeknownst to McCoy. The *Times* wrote, "The engaging grin and the powerful combination punches made him an instant success. More than any other fighter, he started the resurgence of interest here in a sport that had almost died." Boxing fan Richard Orozco recalled Olympic Auditorium promoter Aileen Eaton's relationship with teenage whiz kid Ramos: "That was her boy." Ramos, the two-time lightweight world champion, carried boxing on his shoulders in Los Angeles during the 1960s, much as "Broadway Joe" Namath carried the New York Jets during the same decade. From left to right are McCoy, comanager Lee Prlia (standing), and Ramos.

International Boxing magazine wrote of Long Beach lightweight sensation Mando Ramos, shown entering the ring at the Olympic Auditorium: "Anything can happen with that kid. He's wild, man. Wild! He's also the most exciting thing to happen to boxing since Cassius Clay first opened his mouth." *International Boxing* expounded on Ramos being under 24-hour surveillance as he prepared for his 1969 rematch with champion Teo Cruz: "And, after all, being cooped up in a training camp for over a month is no fun. Mando Ramos must have his fun. Fun follows him wherever he goes. [Manager] Jackie McCoy took no chances. . . . He slept in the same room with Ramos four nights a week, and Lee Prlia, who owns part of Mando's contract, stayed with his investment the other three nights. Ramos had no chance at all to sneak away for a midnight rendezvous." The free-spirited Ramos reminisced, "I miss my girlfriend. I miss the night clubs: Shelly's Manne-Hole and the Lighthouse. What a time I'm going to have when this fight is over." (Photograph by Paul M. Orduna.)

Stylish Mickey Davies of West Virginia was hired as assistant matchmaker to George Parnassus at the Olympic Auditorium in 1959 and promoted to full-time matchmaker in 1965. Davies (background) is pictured in his upstairs corner office with promoter Aileen Eaton and associate matchmaker Don Chargin (foreground, with his back to the camera). All three were key figures responsible for the local boxing revival and development of talent at the Olympic. Boxing columnist Bill O'Neill said, "It was on Mickey's watch that the real ticket-sellers of that decade emerged." (Courtesy of Steve DeBro.)

The documentary *18th & Grand* described Canadian-born Aileen Eaton as "the brilliant promoter and pioneer businesswoman who ran the Olympic Auditorium for almost 40 years." Matchmaker Don Chargin recalled the fierce lightweight match between Mando Ramos and Ultiminio "Sugar" Ramos in 1970, "People on both sides were screaming to stop it. . . . It's the most brutal thing I've ever seen. They sat 10,400 at the Olympic and we had 14,000 people in there. Aileen had a case of Scotch ready for the fire inspector, just in case he walked in."

Besides his duties as matchmaker, Mickey Davies became a color commentator on the weekly television show *Boxing from the Olympic*. Former boxer/historian Rick Farris recalled, "Mickey fit in perfect at ringside on KTLA-TV with Dick Enberg during the first couple years or so, and he loved it." Enberg (right) described Davies (left) in his book, *Oh My!*: "In a sport that is often so cruel and filled with so many vulgar people, Davies was unique. He was charming and gentle and had the demeanor of a professor. He even smoked a pipe." Farris continued, "Once Mickey proved popular as a ringside announcer, he lost interest in being matchmaker, which is a very tough job 50 weeks per year. Mrs. [Aileen] Eaton didn't like that idea and handed Mickey his walking papers." After Davies's 10-year association with the Olympic Auditorium ended in 1969, assistant Don Chargin took over the matchmaker position. Davies's next move was to the Forum as matchmaker (after he was hired by promoters George Parnassus and Don Fraser) before he relocated to the San Diego Coliseum.

Forum boxing director Don Fraser spoke to the *Los Angeles Herald-Examiner*'s Leo Noonan about Ruben Olivares: "In '68, he was more reserved. Now he's a free-wheeling young man who best could be described as one of today's children." Noonan wrote, "In the early years when Olivares [at right in the image at right] was coming to the Forum, he and 'Cuyo' Hernandez [at left in the image at right], his original manager, often quarreled. Both Ruben and Cuyo wanted to be in charge. When Hernandez's contract expired, Hernandez was gone and Ruben officially became his own boss. It has been that way ever since. While Olivares and his present manager, Pancho Rosales, are very close—'like father and son,' says [trainer] Jo Jo Torres—the final decisions always are made by the champion." Below, Olivares (center) is with friends Gene Aguilera (left) and Greg Schultz at the Alexandria Hotel in Los Angeles in 1977.

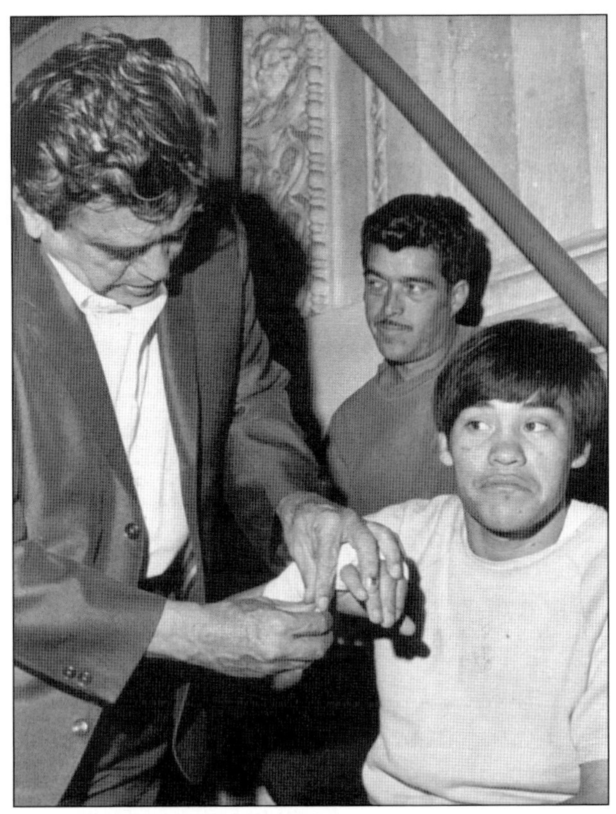

Ring magazine wrote, "The life of Bobby Chacon, in and out of the ring, has always seemed an outlandish drama, pitched to the extremes and filled with promise. When he was 22 years old, he had talent to burn and the style to go with it and he won the world featherweight title. He was a hero in Los Angeles. Just a year later he was considered washed-up, a victim of himself." In 1979, John Beyrooty, of the *Los Angeles Herald-Examiner*, described a Chacon fight-night crowd at the Los Angeles Sports Arena: "The ol' Chacon magic is still there. 'Bob-bee, Bob-bee,' his admirers, who delayed his return trip to the dressing room a full 15 minutes, would scream, 'Bob-bee, Bob-bee.'" *Los Angeles Times* reporter Mark Heisler said, "He was known as 'Schoolboy' Bobby Chacon, the kid from San Fernando High and Cal State Northridge. He was also the WBC's featherweight champion and there was nothing he didn't have going for him. He was pretty and powerful in the ring and he was popular." From left to right are Chacon, Rudy Lopez (owner of the Pasta House), and Carlos Palomino (world welterweight champion).

Alfonso Zamora was the first boxer from Mexico to win an Olympic Games medal as an amateur, then capture a world title belt as a professional. *Los Angeles Times* reporter Jack Hawn wrote, "After winning the silver medal at Munich (1972), Zamora was granted a private audience with then-president Luis Echeverria and was presented with a used automobile." Zamora was also the first boxer in history to win a world title (1975) with a perfect record—20 victories (with 20 knockouts) and no losses. *Boxing Illustrated* magazine screamed the headlines, "New Mexican Star Thrills as WBA King" and "Zamora's Mark Like That of Zorro in Flashily Taking Hong's Crown," and described the flamboyant champion as such: "Right now Alfonso Zamora at 21 is the youngest fighter to ever hold the banty title and for West Coast fight buffs, it is beginning to look like shades of Ruben Olivares all over again." In a bit of pop-culture curiosity, the Soo-Hwan Hong vs. Alfonso Zamora fight poster is shown on the back cover of the Blues Brothers' *Made in America* album (Atlantic Records).

Los Angeles Times sports columnist Jack Hawn wrote of WBA bantamweight champion Alfonso Zamora, "He had money aplenty, a punch that had knocked out every pro he had fought, and with women he was a charmer. At 21, he was floating on a cloud." Zamora, born with a natural killer instinct, was touted by *Boxing Illustrated* as "the good looking Mexican with TNT in both fists." *Sports Illustrated* commented on the epic 1977 "Fight of the Champions" between Alfonso Zamora (right) and WBC bantamweight titleholder Carlos Zarate (left): "Zamora's style is to wade straight in, hooking from both sides. He has been known to drink with equal abandon. Zarate said, 'That's the only edge he has. He's the better drinker.'" After suffering consecutive losses to both Zarate and Jorge Lujan, Zamora disclosed to Fred Robledo of the *Los Angeles Herald-Examiner*, "I wasn't mentally prepared for either fight. I had too many other things on my mind. I had managerial problems. I had family problems. I was going through a separation that led to a divorce."

Bantamweight contender Alberto "Superfly" Sandoval of Pomona was regarded as one of the most classy, charismatic, and fashionable boxers on the West Coast. Manager Jackie McCoy said, "Alberto has as much talent as anyone I've ever handled. He has so much talent it's unbelievable. And, what's most important, he has drawing power. I've seen a lot of great fighters who couldn't fill a telephone booth. Sandoval definitely is not in that category." Sandoval told Dan Hanley of cyberboxingzone.com, "Albert Davila's uncle got me a job in sales at Robert's department store. The press would always take pictures of me in a suit working in the store, which was all good publicity." Hanley concluded, "I find myself blessed these days to be able to recall those brilliant days past in this sport, with one of those memories of a 118-pound, flamboyantly dressed boxer, displaying dazzling looks and hand-speed before a packed house. Of course, you know whom I'm talking about. After all, there was only one Superfly." Sandoval (right) is shown with world bantamweight champion Lupe Pintor (left) and Olympic Auditorium Latino publicist Luis Magana in 1980.

Undefeated WBA bantamweight champion Alfonso Zamora (left) travelled to Sunin Gymnasium in Incheon, South Korea, for his fifth defense in a rematch with former titleholder Soo-Hwan Hong on October 16, 1976. In round 12 (of a scheduled 15), referee Octavio Meyran of Mexico halted the fight due to Hong suffering a broken jaw and badly cut left eye, awarding the victory to Zamora by TKO. The unpopular stoppage in the challenger's country caused a disturbance with the crowd of 15,000, as Hong was ahead on two of the three scorecards. "Fans came into the ring to go after me, but fortunately the police stopped them," Zamora stated, "Hong's brother was furious and began choking the referee, because if the fight goes the distance, Hong gets the decision. At the time, the military ruled because of the tensions between North and South Korea, so for eight hours we were stuck inside the ring because the people wouldn't let us down. Imagine, I was tired, thirsty, and weak and couldn't leave. Nobody knew this, but the whole time my mother was holding my pay, $100,000 in cash, in a bag at ringside." (Courtesy of Frank Aragon.)

Four

The Thin Man of Tepito

Carlos Zarate is a pleasant man outside the ring. Inside the ropes he was tough, adopting a take no prisoners approach. This merciless attitude can be attributed to his upbringing in Tepito, which is one of the roughest areas in Mexico.

—Jack Hirsh in *Ring Sports* magazine

Boxing historian Bert Sugar wrote, "From the moment the matchstick-thin Zarate emerged from one of the barrios outside Mexico City and began striking his opponents with monotonous regularity, he struck a responsive chord in the inmates of those indoor psychiatric wards known as Mexican fight arenas, the Mexican boxing fans, and became at once a symbol and a rarity—a ring killer in a country that loves ring killers and one with an all-perfect record for destruction, racing through his first 23 opponents like a fire extinguisher blowing out candles."

Leo Noonan of the *Los Angeles Herald-Examiner* described the birthplace of Carlos Zarate as such: "[He was] born in one of Old Mexico's shabbiest barrios, the Tepito section of Mexico City. It is the toughest section of the city—fewer live to reach 21 years of age than in any other part of town." Sports editor Allan Malamud stated, "The neighborhood pastime of Tepito, you see, is boxing, fighting. It is the Hell's Kitchen of an era when hooks and jabs are polished in Mexico City, not New York City."

Los Angeles Times writer Earl Gustkey observed, "Zarate has never fit the mold of a boxing champion, he's quiet, impassive, not given to lavish dress or conversation. He doesn't even make predictions." Boxing writer Jack Hirsh noted, "Unlike most big punchers who become vulnerable as the fight progressed, Zarate was a cool ring technician, who knew how to relax and conserve energy."

After losing his WBC bantamweight title in a controversial split decision to stablemate Lupe Pintor in 1979, "El Cañas" Zarate retired, then returned in 1986. Zarate concluded, "I was in the gym regularly all those years. I've had 12 fights since I started my comeback, and I have not disgraced the name of Carlos Zarate. I'm proud of that."

Boxing author Christopher J. Smith perfectly summed up the over-the-weight, nontitle, bantamweight dream match between WBC kingpin Carlos Zarate (left) and WBA champion Alfonso Zamora (right) at the Forum in 1977: "No feeling out, just bombs-away at a high level." In the first round, Zamora jumped right into his destroyer mode, landing solidly on Zarate. With only 52 seconds gone, a crazed male wearing a white tank top with grey shorts, white tube socks, and no shoes jumped into the ring, immediately bringing a touch of controversy to the mega-bout. The interrupter began displaying karate-type moves as the startled combatants looked on until referee Richard Steele halted the action, and the Los Angeles Police Department antiriot squad dragged the interloper out of the ring. Jose Antonio Vazquez De La Torre of *Entre Cuerdas* magazine wrote, "Zamora began landing heavy blows on Zarate, who was saved miraculously by a practitioner of karate." Zarate later admitted, "He hurt me twice, but he didn't hurt me enough. I did not lose my head." Boxing pundits have long since pondered the motives of the mysterious intruder—was it a bizarre coincidence or a well-planned time delay?

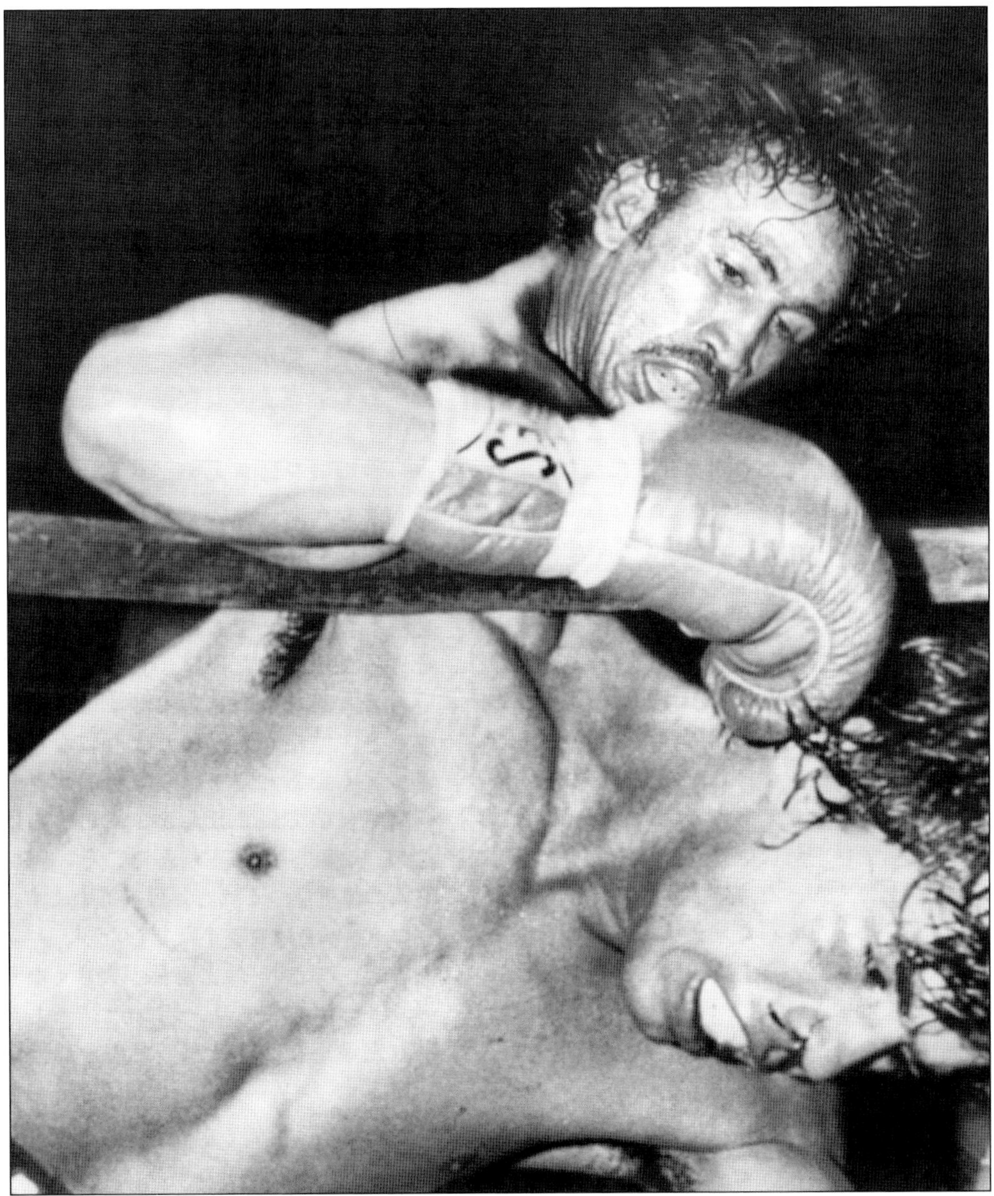

The grand finale came at 1:11 in the fourth round, when Alfonso Zamora (under the rope) lay on the mat bloodied, battered, and knocked out by Carlos Zarate. The bout formally ended when Zamora's father, Alfonso Zamora Sr., threw in the towel that, curiously, landed perfectly across his son's face. Soon thereafter, "Papa" Zamora rushed to the other corner, charging Zarate's manager, Arturo "Cuyo" Hernandez, as both began kicking and punching one another on the ring apron until they were separated by Zarate's trainer, Jo Jo Torres, and security. *World Boxing* magazine reported that Zamora Sr. screamed at Hernandez, "You're a liar and a cheat," believing Hernandez had placed an irritating substance on Zarate's gloves that affected his son's vision. Zamora commented on the "Battle of the Zs" showdown (fought at 119 pounds): "I thought I was doing OK until the third. After that, I don't remember too much. The thing about Zarate is that his punches are so crisp. He has perfect timing." The $401,700 gate was a then-record for "little guys" in a nontitle fight.

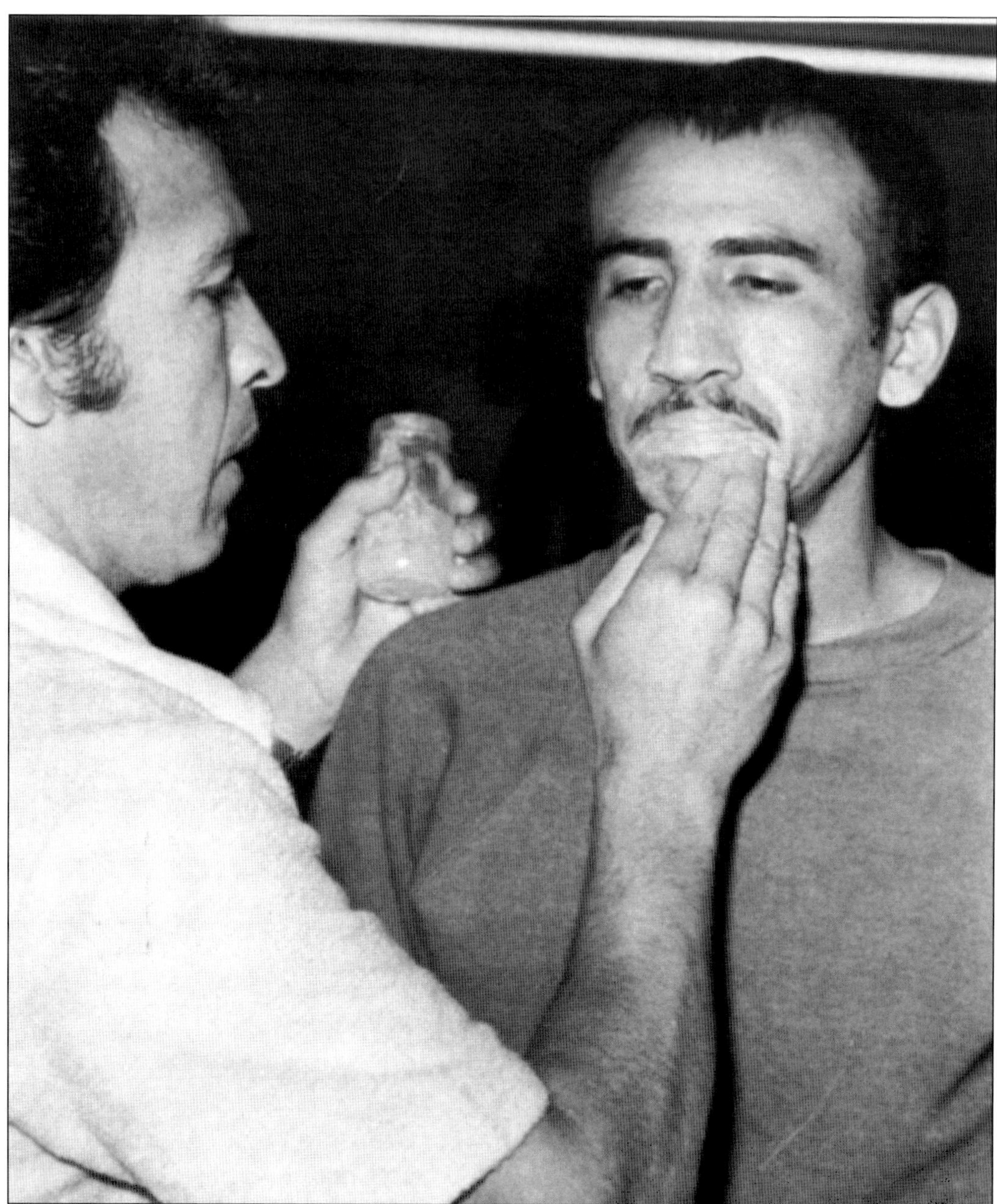

After ravaging through the bantamweight ranks, Mexico City's WBC titleholder Carlos Zarate jumped up a weight class to test his fortunes against WBC super bantamweight champion Wilfredo Gomez. In the storied boxing rivalry between Mexico and Puerto Rico, this fight ranks as one of the most dramatic and controversial. Both Zarate (the 3-to-1 favorite) and Puerto Rico's 122-pound kingpin Gomez entered the ring undefeated, with a combined 72 knockouts out of 74 bouts, making it the highest knockout percentage (98 percent) ever for a world championship fight. Zarate (right) told Jack Hirsh of *Ring Sports*, "We arrived to Puerto Rico on Monday the 23rd of October, 1978. I was in shape and at weight. With five days left until the fight, my brother and trainer, Jorge [left], and I got up early to run. As we left the hotel, it began to rain, and I got soaking wet. When we returned, I began to feel sick but didn't pay that much attention to it."

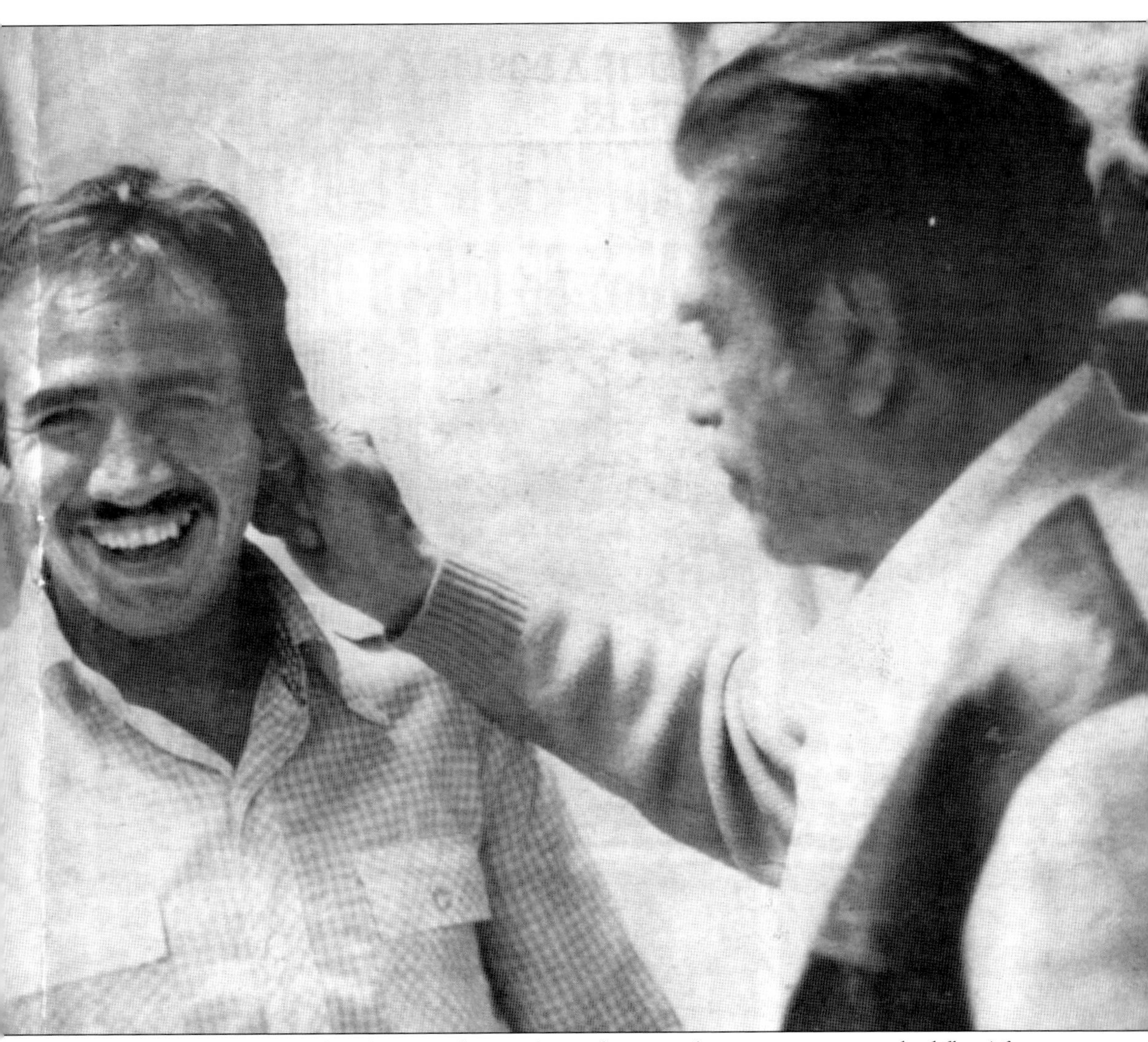

Carlos Zarate (left) recalled, "The next day, my bones began to hurt, turning into a bad flu. After telling my manager, 'Cuyo' Hernandez [right], he said to drink lots of orange juice because of the vitamin C. I was so disappointed with Cuyo because the sugar in the orange juice caused me to gain weight, going up to that of a featherweight. On Thursday, I asked Cuyo to take me to see the WBC doctor because I was hurting. He never took me, and to this day, I still don't know why he acted that way. The day of the weigh-in, which was on the same day of the fight in those days, I was three pounds overweight. I went to the sauna, and later, they put me in a car with heavy clothing with the heater full-on. The Puerto Rican fans outside were screaming 'They're going to kill you, Mexican!' and wanting to flip the car over. I was still slightly overweight and told Cuyo I didn't want to fight."

Carlos Zarate, speaking about his 1978 fight against Wilfredo Gomez, stated, "Cuyo [Hernandez, Zarate's manager] said he spoke to the promoter, and they said if I didn't fight, I would have to indemnify the television network twice what I was going to make. After four tries on the scales, I finally made weight, and had to fight completely weak. Wilfredo could have killed me." In the fourth round, after Zarate was knocked down, Gomez never fully retreated to a neutral corner; as Zarate arose after the mandatory eight-count, Gomez lurked behind referee Harry Gibbs and immediately began attacking without fear of reprisal or disqualification from the referee. *Ring* magazine railed against the arbiter's loss of control: "Pudgy, slow-moving British referee Harry Gibbs [left] was criticized for not preventing Gomez [center] from hitting repeatedly after the bell in the crucial fourth round." WBC president Jose Sulaiman explained, "Gibbs told me he could not hear the bell due to the bedlam of screaming fans." Even announcer Howard Cosell succinctly stated, "Gomez not fighting the cleanest fight in the world, and Gibbs not refereeing the best fight in the world."

Carlos Zarate's older brother, Jorge (pictured in the extreme lower left corner of the image), threw in the towel, signaling an inglorious end to the monumental bout. Zarate recalled, "In those conditions, I lasted five rounds. Gomez took advantage by hitting me when I was on the mat. He knew perfectly well that I was very sick." In an overpowering performance, Gomez (right) knocked down Zarate three times en route to the sixth defense of his title at Roberto Clemente Coliseum in San Juan, Puerto Rico, on October 28, 1978. Zarate reflected, "One afternoon, after training, I found it strange noticing that Mr. Yamil Chade, the representative of Gomez, was starting a close friendship with my manager, Cuyo Hernandez. I know Chade spied and told Gomez everything he saw. I still think that Cuyo and Chade arranged and hatched a plan for me to lose. Everything went against me the moment I arrived in Puerto Rico. It was just a bad fight." Zarate concluded, "I didn't feel good. I wasn't doing good. That's always something I'm always going to have in the back of my head."

Ring magazine reported, "Months before the [1978] fight, Carlos Zarate [above, second from left] and [WBC president] Jose Sulaiman had a long talk about things personal to the champion. 'The truth about Carlos,' Sulaiman says with a sentimental tone, 'is that he really retired before he fought Wilfredo Gomez. He confided to me a long time before the fight, saying he had lost his desire to get up early and run, and to go to the gym each day. He said he could still do it, but that there was no pleasure in it for him. I could see in his eyes that he had pushed himself so hard, trained so diligently, with so much sacrifice, that now, after so many years of hard work, his drive had become stale.'" Below, Zarate (right) is pictured with author Gene Aguilera at the Main St. Gym around 1977.

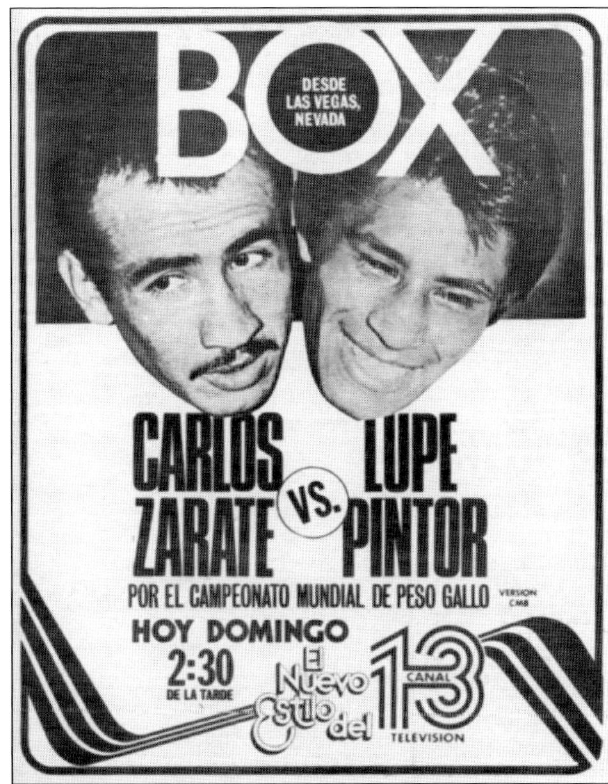

Ring magazine praised WBC bantamweight champion Carlos Zarate: "He was handsome and well-mannered. But it was his extraordinary punching power that was the soul of his fantastic mystique." In his 10th title defense, Zarate (at left in the below image) dropped longtime stablemate Lupe Pintor in the fourth round but still ended up losing the crown in a controversial 15-round split decision. Zarate was offered an immediate rematch but was so angry he abruptly chose to retire. *Ring* described the June 3, 1979, bout at Caesars Palace, Las Vegas, as "one of the worst decisions of the decade. . . . The usually accurate UPI scored the fight 12–3 for Zarate. The former champion's face was filled with shock when the decision was announced. Even tough, little Lupe Pintor, with both eyes nearly shut, appeared dumbfounded when the referee raised his arm."

PESE A LAS PROTESTAS, CURTIDORES PODRIA CONTINUAR EN LA ELIMINATORIA

Zarate ya lo pidió al Consejo Mundial

"QUIERO EL DESQUITE"

ESTO

$6.00

CARA LIMPIA

Dice Pintor

"GANE SINFAVORITISMOS"

LA COMISION DE NEVADA SUSPENDERA A UNO DE LOS JUECES DE LA PELEA

Carlos Zarate is shown in *Esto* newspaper with his facial features virtually unmarked after his rugged 15-round fight against Lupe Pintor (shown in the inset). *Ring* magazine commented, "The next day Zarate issued a bitter statement: 'For some reason I have been robbed of my title by the officials in Nevada. I want the World Boxing Council to study a film of the fight. I should be given my title back. The decision was a terrible disgrace.' It was known that the deposed champion had feuded with his long-time manager, 'Cuyo' Hernandez, who, not incidentally, also handled Pintor. Prior to the fight, the Nevada State Athletic Commission, sensitive to the possibility of chicanery, ordered Hernandez to work neither man's corner. But, following the bizarre verdict, suspicious rumors began to circulate, hinting that a deal had been worked out between all involved. . . . 'The decision could not be changed,' World Boxing Council president Jose Sulaiman said a bit sadly about the controversial outcome. 'I did not agree with it. I scored the fight carefully and had Zarate winning. He outboxed Pintor and knocked him down.'" (Courtesy of *Esto*.)

Five

The Saga of "Little Red"

Danny Lopez looked like a scarecrow with red hair, but his right-hand was loaded with dynamite. He was impassive in the ring, stalking his prey, looking to launch his murderous punch.

—John J. Raspanti of maxboxing.com

Without the muscular, physical attributes of a typical boxer, skinny-armed and -legged Danny "Little Red" Lopez closed his career with a jaw-dropping 39 knockouts out of 42 wins. Don Chargin, veteran matchmaker of the Olympic Auditorium, proudly told *Sports Illustrated* in 1979, "Pound-for-pound, Danny is the hardest puncher in all of boxing today."

Born on the Ute Indian reservation in Fort Duquesne, Utah, Lopez was mired in poverty while growing up in a family of eight children. Lopez disclosed his lineage to Dan Hanley of cyberboxingzone.com: "My father was half [Northern California] Mission Indian and half Mexican. My mother was half Ute Indian and half Irish. Man, it's like I came out of a blender." When Danny was five, his father, Ernest Sr., abandoned the household, leaving his mother, Lucille, to support the family on odd jobs and welfare checks.

Danny spent the first eight years of his childhood hunting rabbits with a bow and arrow while living in a tiny tin-roofed shack with a wood-burning stove and no running water. Subsisting on a diet of powdered eggs, Lopez told *Sports Illustrated*, "My sister Carol and I used to eat sugar sandwiches. We thought that was a great delicacy." No longer able to support her children, their mother turned the brood over to the state, where they were shuffled between several foster homes. The three youngest (Danny, Larry, and Carol) were legally adopted by the Moon family in Jensen, Utah.

A rebellious childhood led to problems for Lopez, resulting in underage drinking, fighting in the streets, and jail time. Little Red talked to Anson Wainwright of *Ring* magazine about turning his life around: "My brother Leonard boxed in the Marines, and my brother Ernie boxed at Stan's Boxing Club [in Orem, Utah]. It was because of them that I wanted to box. I took it up when I was 16."

After being raised in the Utah foster home system, Danny "Little Red" Lopez moved to California at 16 to live with his older brother Ernie "Indian Red" Lopez, already an established and respected welterweight contender. Ernie and his wife, Marcia, had been living in Arcadia, California, since the mid-1960s, having known each other since they attended Orem High School in Utah. Danny, trained by Memo Soto, instinctively followed Ernie's path into the paid ranks of boxing. In a simple twist of fate, teenaged Danny (left) met his future wife, Bonnie Bersik, while she babysat Ernie's four children. The sweethearts got married in 1972 and raised three sons: Bronson, Jeremy, and Dylan. In his professional debut, Danny, 18, was paid $200 for a first-round knockout of Steve Flajole at the Olympic Auditorium on May 27, 1971. To supplement his income, Danny worked at Petrillo's Pizza in San Gabriel, but he left soon after blossoming into a popular Southland featherweight sensation and fan favorite after knocking out 22 of his first 23 opponents.

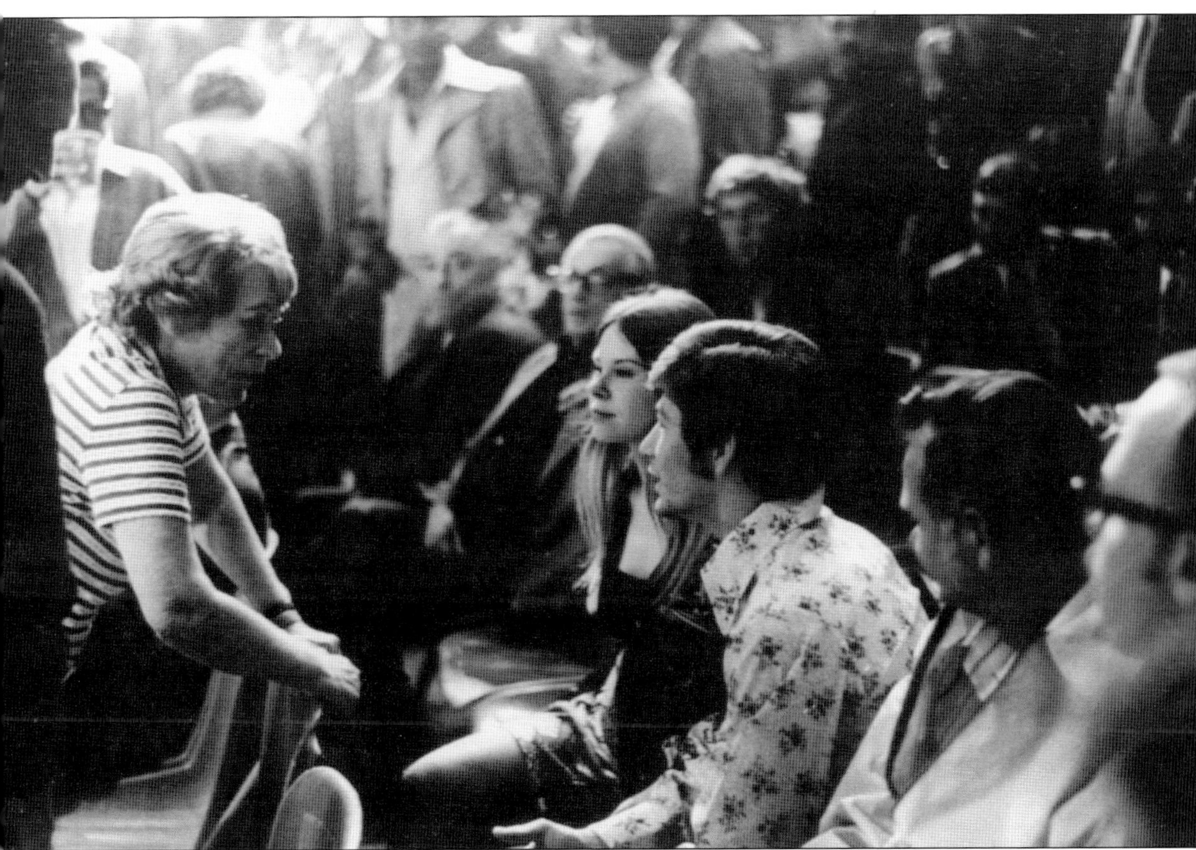

Featherweight champion Danny "Little Red" Lopez recalled to the *Los Angeles Times*, "Those were the days. You saw Albert [Davila] and myself selling out the Olympic time and again. I sold it out, I think, four or five times. It was nice to fight at the Olympic, all that charisma. We were all local heroes." Olympic Auditorium promoter Aileen Eaton (left), shown leaning over to talk to Danny and his wife, Bonnie, said, "Danny Lopez is exciting. You never know when he's going to land one of his haymakers. But I don't think he could learn defense now. It is his instinct to go after a fighter. He gets hit a lot, but he has a tremendous punch." Mike Casey of cyberboxingzone.com wrote, "He possessed that special brand of fighting spirit that sometimes drives a man beyond the boundaries of common sense and safety. You could cut Danny, you could outbox and maybe even outpunch him, but you couldn't destroy his will to win." Seminal singer/songwriter Bob Dylan saluted Little Red in his 1974 composition "Something There Is About You": "There was me and Danny Lopez, cold eyes, black night." (Photograph by George Rodriguez.)

In one of the most grueling West Coast featherweight wars of the 1970s, Danny "Little Red" Lopez faced "Irish" Art Hafey at the Forum on August 6, 1976. Hafey's manager, Suey Welch, said, "In 40 years of watching fighters in Southern California, with all its distractions, I don't believe I ever have seen a cleaner-living, more dedicated one than Art Hafey. The boy's a champ whether or not he ever wins the title." In this 12-round title elimination bout between the two top contenders, a rare 13th round was added in case of a draw. Many of the taller Lopez's blows landed high on the head of the shorter Hafey of San Diego, who went down in the 6th round. "I was groggy," said Hafey. "I would never quit. I could have kept fighting and got hurt. It's no shame to lose to Danny Lopez. The knockdown was some punch." The nonstop-hitting Lopez's victory over the determined Hafey (TKO 7) turned out to be the native Canadian's last fight. Pictured here are, from left to right, Jerry Bilderrain (Hafey's cornerman/chief second), Howie Steindler (Lopez's manager), Hafey, Lopez, and Dick Young (referee). (Photograph by Theo Ehret.)

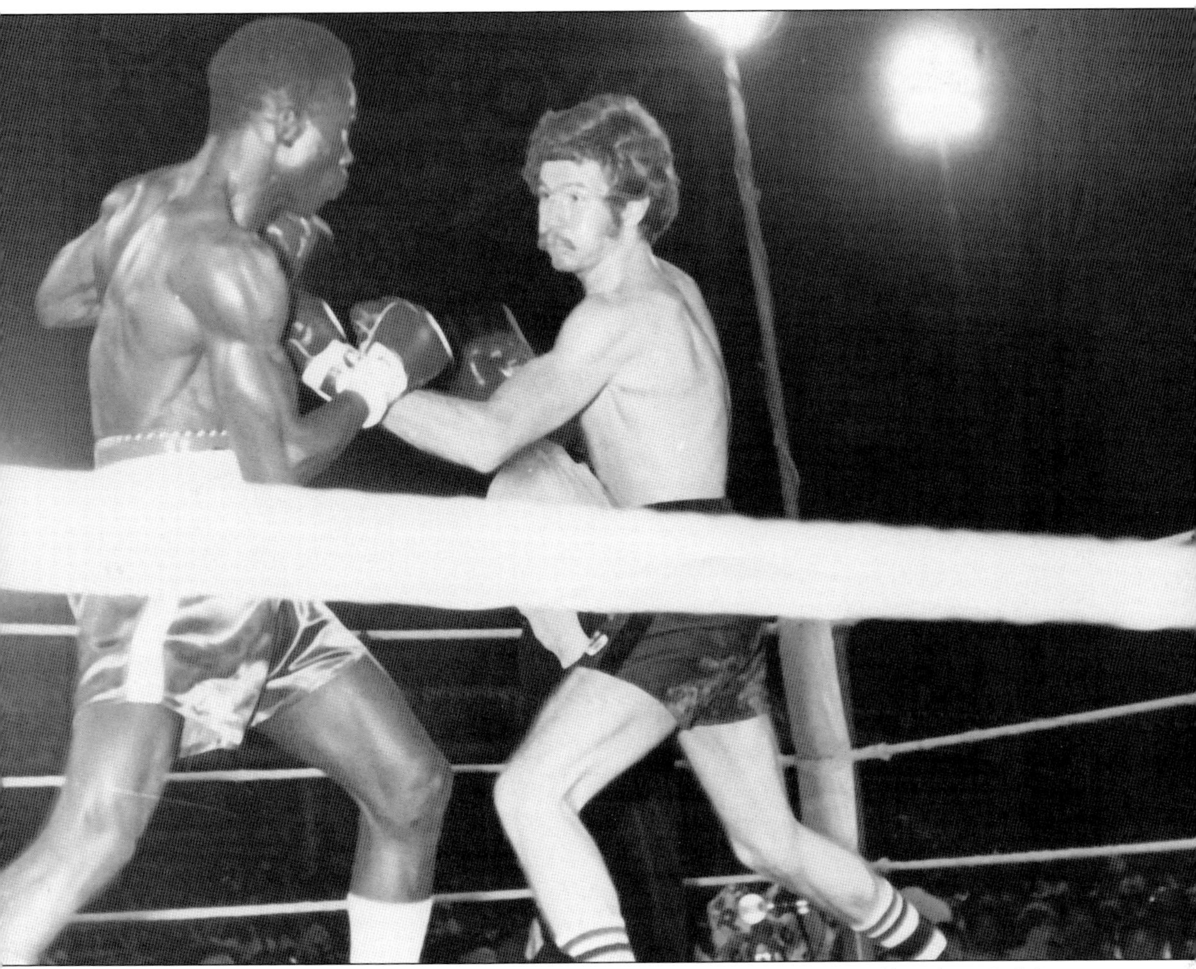

Danny "Little Red" Lopez (right), the slender, redheaded contender from Alhambra, California, travelled halfway across the globe to battle WBC featherweight champion David "Poison" Kotey in his homeland of Accra, Ghana, on November 6, 1976. Kotey, the first professional boxer from Ghana to win a world title, was making the third defense of his crown while being managed by his older brother Daniel, an official with the Ghanaian government in the United Nations. Lopez arrived in West Africa two weeks before the fight to acclimate himself to the tropical heat but was met with less-than-hospitable conditions. Besides staying in an old hotel with no hot water, Lopez suffered intestinal illness from not being accustomed to local food. Little Red sought aid from the US Embassy, US Marines, and Peace Corps volunteers in Accra, recalling, "They got all their food shipped from the United States. So the rest of the time I was there, I drank their water and ate their food." In addition, Lopez was without his manager Howie Steindler, who was under doctor's orders to not fly long distances due to heart problems.

Due to the sweltering West African humidity, Danny "Little Red" Lopez began his daily roadwork at 4:00 a.m. at a local golf course, taking precautions to avoid the alligators in the ponds. At a press conference for the fight, cultural differences were evident when David Kotey stomped on an authentic Native American headdress that Lopez presented to him. Lopez recalled, "Man, that's kind of rude," only to later learn that feathers are sometimes perceived as evil in Ghana. *Sports Illustrated* reported the pressure Lopez felt before the fight when Ghana's president, Gen. Ignatius Acheampong, told him, "You will not leave Ghana with our title." At Accra Sports Stadium, Lopez endured 100 degrees of scorching heat, booming tribal drums, and a deliberate five-hour delay, telling Mike Waters of syracuse.com, "We were supposed to go into the ring at 8 o'clock and we didn't go in until 1 in the morning. I never got an answer for why. Maybe it was a ploy to throw me off. I just sat back and waited and waited." Lopez (right) is shown exchanging blows with Kotey during their second fight in 1978.

Danny "Little Red" Lopez recalled the huge, fervent David Kotey crowd (the second-largest in boxing history) going silent when the judges' scorecards were read. "When they announced I had won the title [UD 15], you could hear 15 Americans stand up and cheer for me out of 100,000 people in the soccer stadium." Kotey, dropped by Lopez in the 11th round, had to be hospitalized after the fight, requiring 37 stitches to repair his nose and lower lip. African authorities were so upset that they blocked all media from releasing the news. *Sports Illustrated* reported, "It took nearly two days for the word to get back to [Howie] Steindler in Los Angeles that his fighter was the world champion." After reviewing tapes of the fight, Lopez noticed another key advantage for Kotey: "I timed the rounds, and every time Kotey was about to go down, that round would be shorter than it was supposed to be. One round was only two minutes long." Lopez is shown celebrating after defeating Kotey (TKO 6) in a rematch bout at the Hilton Hotel in Las Vegas in 1978 as referee Ray Solis (left) looks on.

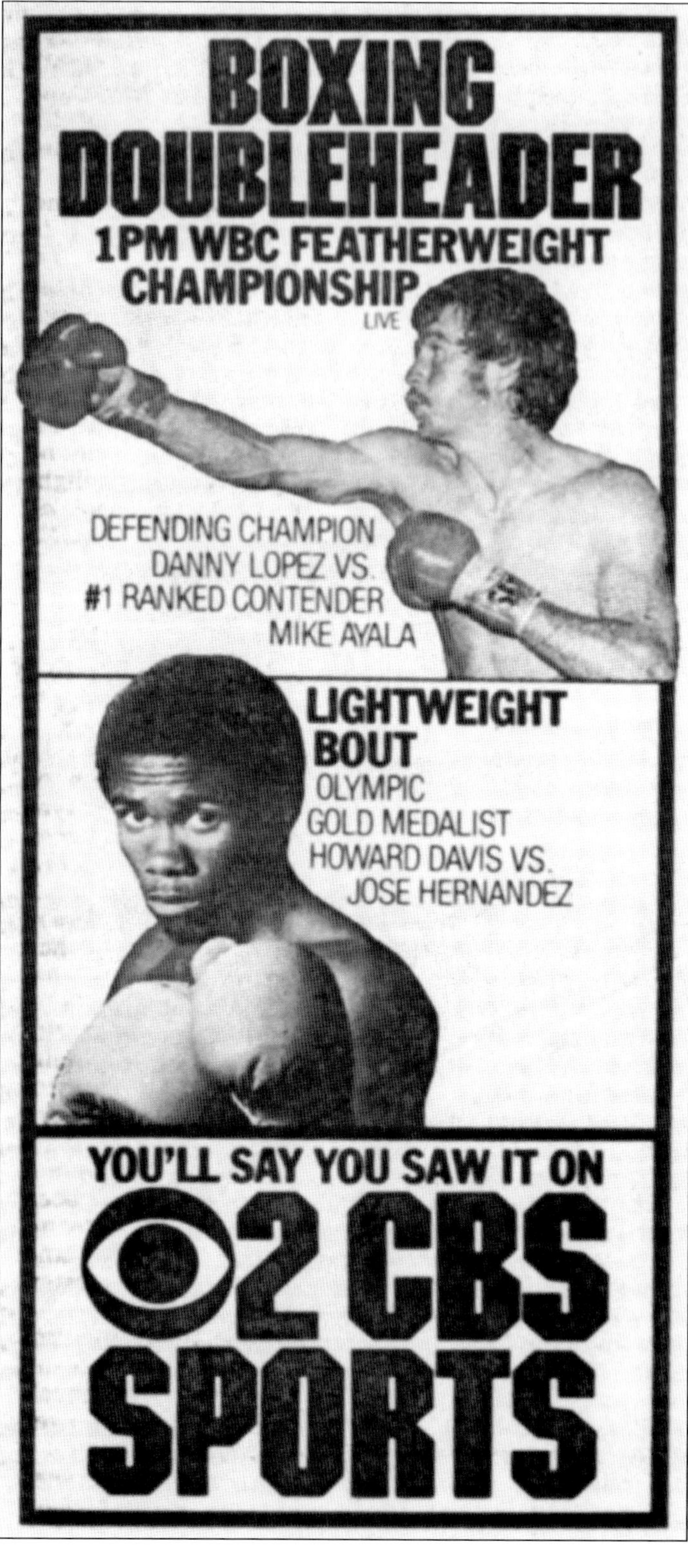

Danny "Little Red" Lopez's seventh defense of his WBC featherweight title versus NABF featherweight champion Mike "El Ciclon" ("The Cyclone") Ayala was held in front of 15,000 screaming fans at the San Antonio Convention Center Arena on June 17, 1979. Lopez's manager, Howie Steindler, once said, "Danny doesn't care who or where he fights. You could put him in a river of piranhas in the middle of the jungle and he wouldn't complain." In Lopez's toughest challenge yet, held in Ayala's backyard, Bill Merriman (anointed "the undisputed king of ring announcers" by the *San Antonio Express-News*) issued one of boxing's most dramatic and frenzied introductions of all time. A local boxing fan stated that the CBS-TV nationally televised bout "melted into one 15-round brutality fest," featuring the relentless Lopez against the smaller Ayala—the oldest of a phenom family of boxing brothers, followed by Sammy, Tony Jr., and Paulie. Ayala continually counterpunched off the ropes, but in the seventh round, a powerful Lopez combination caught El Ciclon, who fell to one knee in a delayed reaction, causing boxing trainer Angelo Dundee to comment on the air, "I think his nose is broke, that's why he went down slow."

The 11th round of the 1979 Lopez-Ayala fight was a sheer spectacle of controversy. After Danny "Little Red" Lopez (left) dropped Mike Ayala with a left hook for the second time in the bout, referee Carlos Padilla misinterpreted the timekeeper's 10-count, erroneously counted Ayala out, and declared Lopez the winner. This prompted CBS sportscaster Tim Ryan to excitedly state, "And wait a minute! The fight is not over! The referee Padilla had counted him out, but the timekeeper and the WBC representative Dr. Romeo Garcia, of Mexico, are saying the count had not reached 10." A fight fan commented on "the infamous round wherein Ayala presumably got up after the 10-count, was declared the loser, his corner protested, then referee Carlos Padilla ordered everyone to get out of the ring and to let the fight continue. It was funny to see Ayala get KO'd twice in the same fight. You don't see that very often." Boxing commentator/trainer Gil Clancy was shocked at the overruling, saying, "This is a first for me. I've never seen this before!"

Angelo Dundee spoke of the manner in which Danny "Little Red" Lopez (left) systematically broke down Mike Ayala all night: "There's that right-hand to the body I'm talking about. It sounds like a gun exploding when he hits him there." Lopez's left-hook knockout of Ayala provided the perfect ending to the slugfest, heralded by ring announcer Bill Merriman shouting into the microphone, "One minute, nine seconds of the 15th round, winner and still featherweight champion of the world, Danny 'Little Red' Lopez . . . Lopez!" The epic battle was unfortunately marred by the post-fight disclosure of Ayala's troubles with drugs, as he told UPI sportswriter Logan Hobson that the Lopez fight was something he "wasn't mentally ready for." Ayala continued, "I had a drug problem. I was immature. I had a dominant father [Tony Sr.]. It was hard coping at first. I became my own man. I stopped using heroin and kicked [the habit]." The Lopez vs. Ayala ring war took place in front of the largest crowd in San Antonio boxing history and was selected as 1979's "Fight of the Year" by *Ring* magazine.

After a disappointing rematch loss to WBC featherweight champion Salvador Sanchez in 1980, Danny "Little Red" Lopez retired from boxing at the age of 27. The grueling ring battles Lopez experienced took their toll, and he soon embarked on a new career doing demolition work for an El Monte cement contractor. Inspired by comeback king George Foreman and his multimillion-dollar paydays, Lopez, 39, told *Los Angeles Times* sportswriter Steve Springer, "If he can do it, I can do it. But Father Time takes your reflexes away from you." Lopez returned to the ring to recapture some of that old magic, recalling, "I missed the life. This construction work is tough. I figured if I was going to be working this hard, I may as well be in the gym doing something I know." Lopez reminisced on his epic 1974 clash with fellow West Coast rising boxing sensation Bobby Chacon, "Bobby and I could have had the millions if we fought now. Then, I wouldn't have to be working my buns off in construction." Lopez is shown sitting in his corner while being attended to by trainer Memo Soto (left) and manager Bennie Georgino (right).

After a 12-year absence from boxing, a ring-rusty Danny "Little Red" Lopez (42–5) attempted an ill-fated comeback against Temple City journeyman Jorge Rodriguez, who sported a record of 10 wins, 27 losses, and 2 draws (including losing 14 out of his last 15 fights). Earl Gustkey, of the *Los Angeles Times*, wrote of Lopez's February 27, 1992, bout at the Irvine Marriott Hotel, "Seconds into the first-round, a very ordinary, hand-picked opponent, Jorge Rodriguez, was hitting Lopez at will." Promoter Roy Englebrecht said, "His last fight ever was with us. . . . We had a standing-room-only crowd on its feet for his introduction. Incredible moment. It turned bittersweet because we matched him against a very average opponent. His speed was gone and he didn't make it out of the second round." Lopez, without an offensive attack that disastrous evening, spoke to *Deseret News* about his second-round TKO loss: "It was something I had to know, or I'd have been kicking myself ever since, if I didn't try it."

Six

They Called Him . . . "Tweety"

I had a great-aunt who gave me that nickname as a kid and it stuck throughout my career and even until now. I guess the reference is like the cartoon. You know, big head and a little body.

—Alberto "Tweety" Davila, former WBC bantamweight world champion, as told to Dan Hanley of cyberboxingzone.com

Alberto Davila was born in Olton, Texas (near Lubbock) on August 10, 1954, but raised 30 miles northwest in Dimmitt. When Alberto was 12, his parents, Proculo "Joe" and Sabina, moved to Pomona, California, with their family of 11 children. Alberto's wife, Roberta, said of his moniker, "In a nutshell . . . his aunt's mother (she's his aunt through marriage) came to see him as a newborn. She lovingly exclaimed, 'Mira, como un Tweety Bird!' ('Look, like a Tweety Bird!'). His mom says he was thin, large blue eyes, with wispy blond hair. The nickname stuck to this day."

Staff writer Richard Hoffer of the *Los Angeles Times* described the mild-mannered Davila "as more of a craftsman than a brawler, a boxer who embodied all the best aspects of the so-called sweet science." Known as quiet, intelligent, and dedicated, Davila said, "I've always been clean. I get such a natural high when I work out, I feel so good. I don't need drugs. I've never had any problems. I go to schools and speak to the kids, tell them to work hard and don't do drugs."

After making the first successful defense of his WBC bantamweight title against Enrique Sanchez in 1984, Davila ruptured a disc in his back while pulling out a bush next to his house. Davila recalled this bit of misfortune, "I didn't know how seriously I hurt myself, but one day I was training and I threw a punch and I hit somebody and the pain just shot down my legs. I couldn't even walk. I couldn't even tie my shoes." After Davila's successful back surgery, the *Los Angeles Times* noted, "That cost him a year and the title, which was stripped while he rehabilitated."

Alberto "Tweety" Davila was known as a devoted family man and a gentleman in and out of the ring. However, as fight-time neared, Alberto's wife, Roberta, spoke to *Boxing Illustrated* of how her husband's demeanor quickly changed. "Tweety can sometimes be sort of edgy the week of a fight, so I tell Gabriel [their son] not to do anything that might make him a little nervous." Alberto remembered, "Training for a fight was the toughest thing. Here I was, a young guy, separated from my family for two weeks in a hotel room, all alone. I remember being so thirsty, so hungry. Before a fight, a fighter is like an animal, a time bomb. I became another person. I was happy when the fight was over because then I got to be a normal person again. A human being wanting to see everyone living in one big happy world." Davila (center) is shown at the Main St. Gym in 1980 with stablemates Jaime Garza (left) and Oscar "The Boxer" Muniz as he prepared for his title fight against Lupe Pintor. (Photograph by Linda Platt.)

Alberto Davila recalled, "Lupe Pintor and I fought on the same show one night, and my wife, Roberta, saw him fight. She was so impressed, she just loved the way he fought. So, then one day I told her, 'Hey, I'm fighting Pintor.' She didn't tell me nothing but she got so scared because she knew I was in for a hard fight." The *Long Beach Press-Telegram* wrote, "Davila, a 3–1 underdog, stood fast against Pintor's heavier punching and eventually wore his man down," resulting in a 10-round unanimous decision victory for Davila at the Forum on February 25, 1976. In a textbook display of outhustling Pintor, Davila said, "I fought a beautiful fight that night and beat him." Davila related to boxing writer Dan Hanley, "Oh, he was mad over that fight too. I ruined the party for him. Do you know he wouldn't even talk to me after that." Reigning WBC bantamweight champion Pintor (right) of Mexico City is shown rallying down the stretch in a close victory (MD 15) over Davila (in his third title try) at Caesars Palace, Las Vegas, on December 19, 1980.

Alberto Davila reflected on his July 19, 1976, loss (TKO 9) to future champion Wilfredo Gomez in San Juan, Puerto Rico: "Let me tell you what went on at the weigh-in. I weigh in fully clothed at 117. He is stark naked and they announce him at 121 and he quickly grabs a cup of something and downs it before we can even look at the scale. This way he doesn't have to weigh in again. I have no idea what he actually weighed. As for the fight, after the first round I thought to myself, 'I'm in for a long night!'" Davila told the *Los Angeles Times*, "I loved the sport. I loved competing. I loved what it did for me. Boxing was good to me. It gave me a sense of pride and it let me see parts of the world that I might never have seen if I hadn't been a fighter. It's a hard sport. You've got to love it and I did. As dirty as it is, I miss it dearly. But I'm very happy away from it—the corruption, the bad people." From left to right are Don Georgino (Five Star Promotions president), Davila, Danny Lopez, and Bennie Georgino (manager). (Photograph by Linda Platt.)

Bantamweight Alberto Davila recalled the strategy to make himself more marketable to the growing Latino audience at the Olympic Auditorium: "The name on my birth certificate says Albert Davila. But when I first started out boxing professionally, my manager Howie Steindler and I decided to change my first name to Alberto. We thought we could get the Mexican boxing fans on our side, but as it turns out, when I started beating their guys, they booed us anyway." From left to right are John Montes (trainer), Davila, Bennie Georgino (manager), and Jackie McCoy (cornerman). (Photograph by Carlos Baeza.)

Ring announcer Jimmy Lennon Sr. (left) raises the hand of jubilant new bantamweight champion Alberto Davila as Davila's wife, Roberta, and manager Bennie Georgino (behind Davila) congratulate him after defeating Francisco "Kiko" Bejines at the Olympic Auditorium on September 1, 1983. The persistent Davila achieved his goal of becoming world champion in his fourth try at the title, but the facial expressions of John Montes Sr. and WBC president Jose Sulaiman (in the background) foretell the serious extent of Bejines's fatal injuries. (Photograph by Carlos Baeza.)

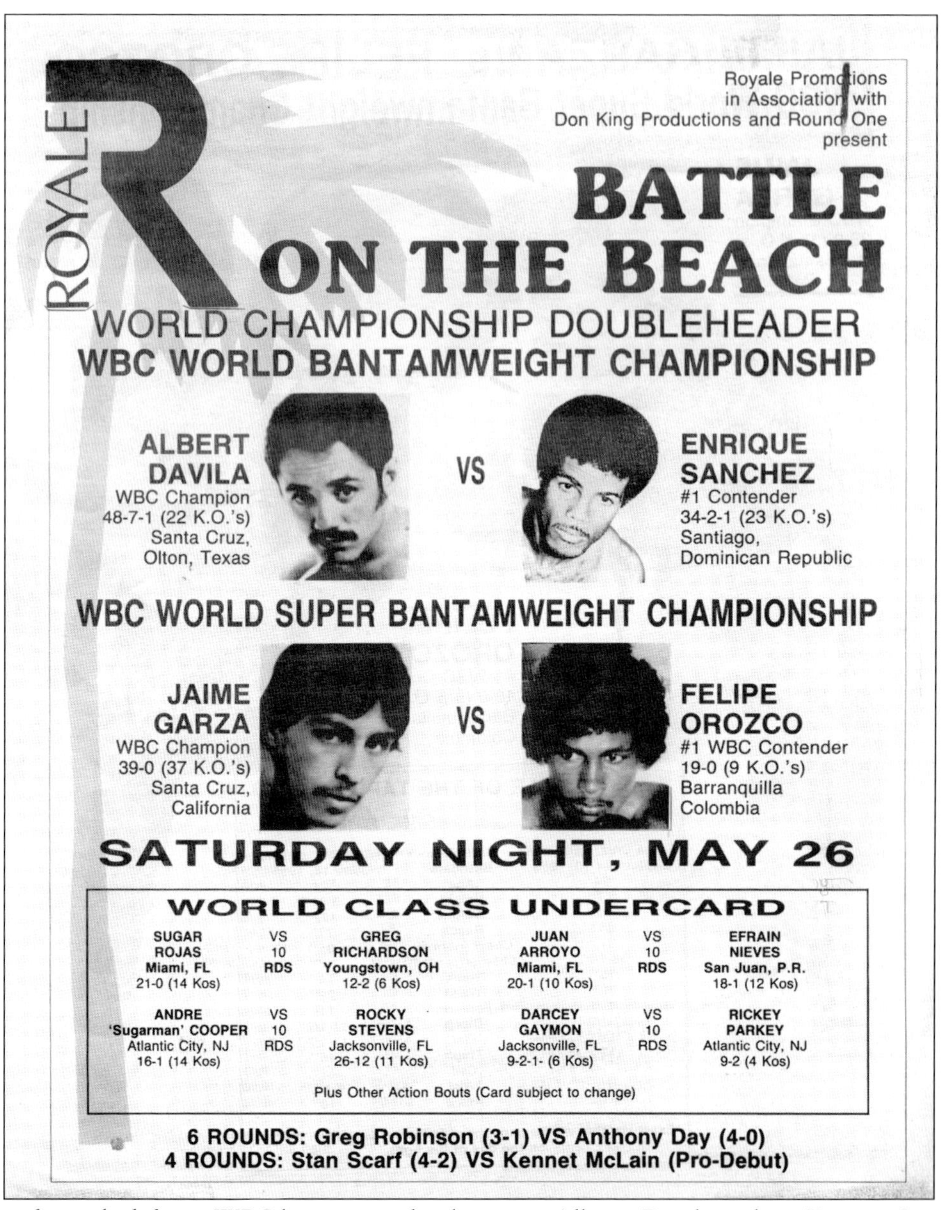

For his first title defense, WBC bantamweight champion Alberto Davila took on Enrique Sanchez of the Dominican Republic in the Art Deco District of Miami Beach (between Twelfth and Fourteenth Streets) on May 26, 1984. Davila recalled the "Battle on the Beach" (also known as the "Battle of the Monsoon"): "We had a boxing ring put on the beach right there on the sand. They had seats all around it and they put a tarp over the ring. Well, in the seventh round it started raining, the wind started blowing so hard, that the rain was coming down sideways, coming into our angle. I was facing the rain and it was stinging my face, and it was hurting. So, I turned Sanchez into the rain and had the rain hitting his face, besides my gloves. So, it worked out beautiful. The rain revived me during the fight, but I was in great shape anyway." Davila spoke to writer Dan Hanley about the heavenly assist, "Sanchez was a little ahead at the time and the fight turned at this point. I stopped him in the 11th-round (TKO) and told the press it was the 'Holy Water' from above."

Bantamweight Frankie Duarte (at right in the above image) explained to Jim Murray of the *Los Angeles Times* how badly out of shape he was for his first fight with Alberto Davila (at left in the above image, with Danny Lopez in the center playing referee) at the Olympic Auditorium in 1977: "You might say Davila took me out in the fifth round, but I took myself out." Davila (at right in the below image), in turn, spoke of their 1987 bloodbath battle at the Forum, which ended as a controversial TKO win for Duarte, "What a robbery! This wasn't even close. I dropped him and was way ahead. I picked up a cut from a butt and they stop it in the 10th. I pleaded with [referee] Lou Filippo and [California State boxing official] Marty Denkin because they had to have known what caused the cut. But the stoppage stood."

Alberto "Tweety" Davila travelled far and wide to regain his title, meeting WBC bantamweight champion Miguel "Happy" Lora in front of 50,000 fervent fans in Barranquilla, Columbia, on November 15, 1986. Davila recalled the losing effort (UD 12): "It was frustrating because he caught me in the first round and broke my nose. I was bleeding the whole time. The guy was just running around, taunting me, he never stopped to fight. I was chasing him. That was the only time in my whole career where I wanted to quit, but my heart didn't let me. I hated his style. I never caught him. I'm sure he was higher than a kite over there." Two years later, Davila (left) again challenged Lora unsuccessfully (UD 12) for the title at the Forum. Davila said, "I remember telling my corner after the fifth round, I'm gonna knock this fool out. But he comes out the next round, fresh again. After the fight, they took two vials of his urine [for antidoping testing]. The first one came out dirty, the second one came out dirtier. That was my last fight."

Seven

The Latin Style Arrives

I represent for my people 110 percent. When I step into the ring, I want the other person at the other side of the ring, whether he's Black, Puerto Rican, to know he's going to fight a real Mexican that's not afraid to go to war. And I think that's what people like.

—Fernando Vargas, super welterweight world champion, speaking to *OYE* magazine in 2000

This chapter will showcase the Latino/Mexican American/Chicano boxers from the West Coast who excelled by using their fists to rise up from the mean streets of the barrio. By bringing their hard work, excitement, and dreams to the ring, they made a better life for themselves and their families.

Teddy Atlas, trainer and fight commentator, recalled the Mexican style of boxing: "They're looking to hurt you. Their thought isn't really that they're looking to outbox you. They're looking to do it the old-fashioned way. By hitting you harder than you hit them." Boxing historian and author Bert Sugar heralded the arrival of a new style of Latino boxer: "Today there is no such thing as a Latino 'face-first' fighter, their skills such that they combine traditional 'machismo' with boxing 'smarts.'"

In *Latino Legends*, artist LeRoy Neiman recognized the emotions the Latino heritage brings to the table: "They follow an entourage down the aisle to the ring that form a procession. It's like a religious ritual. Handlers carry championship belts aloft like relics of a saint. Upon entering the ring, they will kneel in their corner and pray, and at the sound of the opening bell, make the sign of the cross. It's for real. God must pay heed, because there sure have been enough Latino world champions."

Boxing writer David A. Avila reflected on the undying pride the fans wear on their sleeves: "When two Latino fighters engage in a mega-fight, you can expect their fans to arrive with large flags, banners, and wearing clothing representing their nation's colors. They shout, scream, and cry over their heroes, and for this reason, Latino prizefighters bring a passion to the sport like no others."

After holding the NABF lightweight belt in 1970 and challenging for the world title on three occasions, Ruben Navarro proudly proclaimed, "I put Maravilla on the map." Steve DeBro of the documentary *18th & Grand* wrote, "Ruben Navarro, 'The Maravilla Kid' from East L.A., made his professional debut in 1967, coming up in the midst of the Chicano movement. He told us he felt both pride and pressure, fighting not just for himself, but for his people." Navarro, a graduate of Garfield High School, remembered, "My parents couldn't afford to send me to college, so the only way to get out was through boxing. Carrying 'La Raza' on my back was a huge responsibility, and it's a responsibility that isn't really given to you. You don't have a choice in the matter, you just do it and that's it. They pushed me. They want you to succeed, and the more pressure I put on myself, the better boxer I became. It's a heavy load to carry the weight of the Chicano community because I didn't want to let anyone down. 'La Raza' made me who I am."

Ernie "Indian Red" Lopez, a rugged welterweight contender fighting out of Arcadia, California, was the older brother of world featherweight champion Danny "Little Red" Lopez. After winning the California welterweight title with a seventh-round knockout of Andy Gonzalez on July 6, 1967, at the Olympic Auditorium, one month later, Lopez travelled on his only trip to Japan to meet Musashi Nakano in a title elimination bout. Lopez notched a third-round knockout over Nakano, with the *Los Angeles Times* reporting, "In 1967, Lopez wore an Indian chief's headdress into the ring in a match against Musashi Nakano in Japan. Lopez said, 'I bought the thing at Disneyland to take over with me. . . . I liked it so much I was going to keep it. But it turned out they have this custom in Japan where the fighters exchange gifts before the fight. Nakano gave me a samurai warrior's jacket, and I gave him the headpiece.'" In this photograph, Lopez (left) playfully threatens to scalp rival Hedgemon Lewis with a tomahawk. (Photograph by Theo Ehret.)

Off to a fast start, Ruben Navarro (12–0–1) signed to meet reigning 130-pound world super featherweight champion Hiroshi Kobayashi in a nontitle fight at Korakuen Hall in 1968. Navarro recalled to Dan Hanley of cyberboxing.com: "We accepted the fight in Japan to fight Kobayashi because they thought I'd be an easy fight. When the sparring partner they gave me began reporting back that I was going to beat Kobayashi, they started playing games with me. One night after dinner, I came back to my room and they had a naked blonde waiting there for me in the room. Anything to break me down. Now, this was not business. I was the one who was going to get hit in that ring, and I threw her out. When the blonde didn't work, they said I couldn't use my protective cup. They gave in when we said we were leaving. But you know, I was honored that they thought so highly of me that they would pull these stunts. And they were right, because I beat him good over 10 rounds." Navarro is shown hitting the double-end bag at the Main St. Gym as trainer Al Silvani looks on.

Raised in a boxing family, lightweight Petey "Schoolboy" Vital of Montebello, California, grew up with his young siblings at the Main St. Gym under the strict eye of owner Howie Steindler and trainers Arthur "Duke" Holloway and Thomas "Rip" Roseboro. A sign on the wall read, "Please do not bring children under eight years old in the gym. We don't want anyone smarter than us in here." Petey's sister Martha recollected, "We were the only kids that Howie let into his office." Petey said, "My grandfather was a fighter. My father was a fighter. In fact, the day I was born, my father fought his fifth professional fight. I've been at it a long time. I don't know how to do anything else but the fight game." His father/manager Pete Vital Sr. (left) fought under the tutelage of Los Angeles boxing idol Enrique Bolanos, but Petey (right) recalled, "My mom [Delia] taught me how to jab." Closing with 19 wins (4 knockouts), 10 losses, and 4 draws, Petey reflected on his career (1969–1975) to the *Hawaii Tribune-Herald*: "I was 24 years old, but I started at 17 years old. I was already tired." (Courtesy of Martha Vital.)

HARBOR VS MARAVILLA

MANDO *(Los Angeles)* **10 RDS - NO TV** *(Los Angeles)* **RUBEN**

RAMOS vs NAVARRO

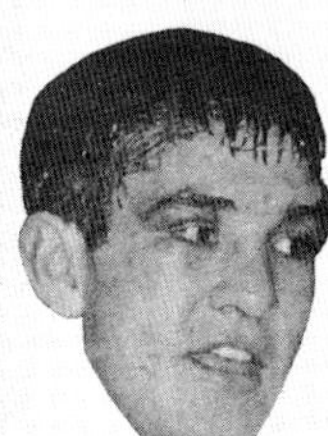

THUR. Nite SEPT. 30

OLYMPIC AUD

Mando: No. 2 Wants to regain Title **Ticket Prices: Ringside $15.00, Lower Balcony $15.00, Upper Balcony $10.00** Ruben: No. 4, "I'll KO Mando"

PROMOTER: AILEEN EATON **MATCHMAKER: DON CHARGIN**

42 COLBY POSTER PRINTING CO., 1332 W. 12th Place, L. A. 9001

Ruben Navarro recalled to writer Dan Hanley, "Mando [Ramos] and I were always going back and forth in the press." Navarro hyped his upcoming fight with the former lightweight champion to the dailies, "Ahh, Mando's not in shape, he's been training in bars. I know, because I was with him!" Navarro expressed to writer/photographer Rudy Rodriguez, "Sometimes I feel a little bit resentful because of all the attention Ramos gets, but he's the champ—so I guess he's got it coming." The *Los Angeles Herald-Examiner* wrote of the rivalry, "Ramos selected Navarro as a tuneup partner for his Madrid bout with Pedro Carrasco. They met at the Olympic in September [1971] after Mando had been idle 10 months. Navarro said, 'You saw what happened, I beat him. It wasn't right for him to get the decision. He got it because he's Mando and they don't care about me. Mando knows I licked him, too. He has admitted it to me. Every time I see him I remind him of it. He tells me we'll get it on again. But when?'"

FORUM BOXING INC.

presents

ALL STAR BOXING

Every Monday Night at 8 pm

The "Chicano Rat Pack" (Mando Ramos, Raul Rojas, and Ruben Navarro) was a mischievous trio of rogues known for partying together as well as fighting each other. Navarro disclosed to writer Dan Hanley, "Well, to tell you the truth, yeah, we all drank, smoked pot, and did cocaine, but I only did it after a fight, whereas they were doing it all the time." Sportswriter Tomas Benitez described the sentiment of the East Los Angeles fight crowd when Navarro (right) took on Frankie Crawford (left) in a grudge match at the Olympic Auditorium in 1971: "But everybody was for Navarro, because of what Crawford had been saying about Mexican fighters." Navarro concluded, "As for the fight with Frankie, we would all hype a fight, but he went a little too far . . . he went around telling the press that I pulled a knife on him and such. He really angered me for the fight, and I gave him a good licking for it. I was even warned by the referee for holding him up."

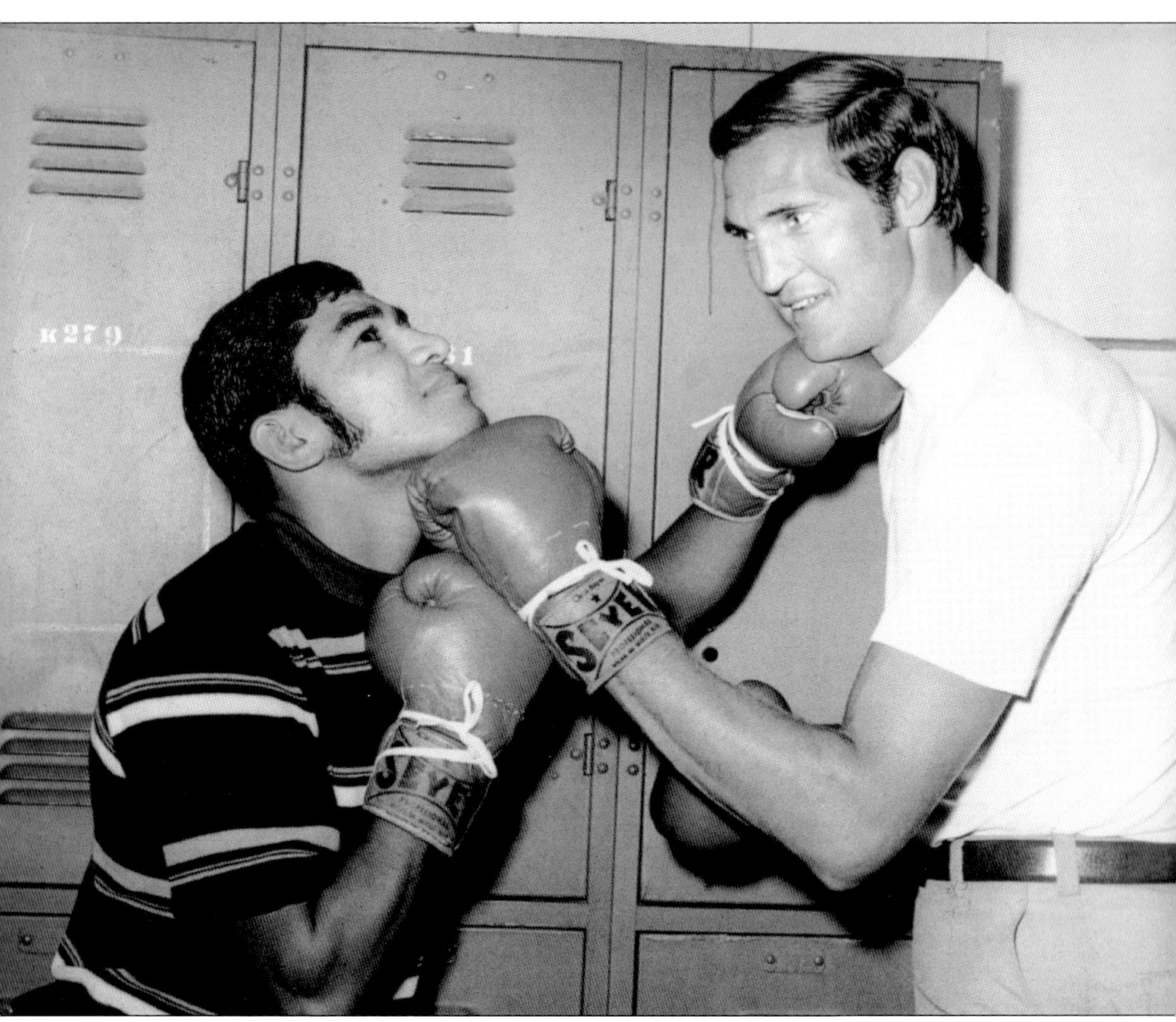

Doug Krikorian of the *Los Angeles Herald-Examiner* wrote, "In the late sixties and early seventies, Ruben Navarro was a member of the Three Musketeers that cut a legendary path on the local boxing scene. His partners, of course, were Raul Rojas and Mando Ramos. It was their passionate credo to never turn down a drink, a woman, a joint, a party invitation, or a loan request from a friend. Their feats outside a ring were even more incredible than their feats inside it, which weren't bad considering Rojas became the featherweight champion, Ramos the lightweight champion, and Navarro the No. 1 challenger. They spent most of their nights in the arms of well-endowed, eager young ladies, hopping from bar to bar, pursuing the endless gratitude of fame, drinking themselves into a stupor." Navarro (left), shown playfully sparring with Los Angeles Lakers star Jerry West, said, "I was making more than 50,000 bucks a year. That wasn't bad dough for a kid 26 years old who grew up on the East Side." (Photograph by Theo Ehret.)

Pictured above are, from left to right, Ralph Gambina (boxing manager), Oscar "Shotgun" Albarado (WBC/WBA super welterweight champion), Vic Weiss (manager of Armando Muniz), Connie Stevens (actress/singer), unidentified, and Armando "The Man" Muniz (welterweight contender) at the International Youth Boxing Club's (IYBC) 1974 annual awards dinner at the Biltmore Hotel in downtown Los Angeles. Sportswriter Bill O'Neill described the undefeated Muniz's (12–0) first big-money bout of his career against Albarado (35–4), of Uvalde, Texas: "It was 10 rounds of raw, blood-and-guts action, as the two Mexican gamesters battered away at each other in an alley fight that recalled the Carmen Basilio–Tony DeMarco wars of 1955." Below, Muniz (right) fights to a draw with future champion Albarado in their battle at the Olympic Auditorium on May 6, 1971. (Both, courtesy of Armando Muniz.)

The crime of the century occurred in 1975 in the title bout between WBC/WBA welterweight champion Jose "Mantequilla" Napoles and challenger Armando "The Man" Muniz in Acapulco, Mexico. With Napoles unable to continue in the 12th round due to the bloody, one-sided beating administered by Muniz, referee Ramon Berumen awarded a horrendous technical decision victory to Napoles, incredulously stating the cuts to the champion were caused by Muniz head-butts in the 3rd round. In the quickly mandated rematch, held four months later, Muniz had problems acclimating to the high altitudes of Mexico City, while Mantequilla adjusted his fight plan to pull out a 15-round unanimous decision victory at Palacio de los Deportes. Muniz's wife, Yolanda, recalled, "I had been sitting in the fourth row behind the brother of Mexico's president Luis Echeverria. He took a silver Rolex watch off his wrist and passed it down to me, saying, 'Please give this to Armando. He is a great boxer. Congratulations.'" Yolanda concluded, "It was an honoring gift." In this image, Yolanda (right) holds daughter Alice while Armando holds son Armando Jr. at their home in Monterey Park, California, in 1972. (Courtesy of Yolanda Muniz.)

At the conclusion of the second fight between Jose "Mantequilla" Napoles and Armando "The Man" Muniz, Muniz's wife, Yolanda, overheard Mexican actress Carmen Salinas crudely shout out to Mantequilla, "Ay *esta la vieja de Muniz*" ("There's Muniz's old lady"). Yolanda continued, "Napoles came down off the ring, jumped over a few rows, and extended his hand to greet me. At least that's what I thought he was going to do. As I extended my hand to meet his, he flipped it up, making the number-one symbol, and shouted, '*¡Sigo siendo número uno!*' ('I'm still number one!'). I immediately cramped up. At Armando's fights, I never shout, never disrespect anyone, I'm not that type of person. But this time, I was shocked over Napoles's behavior [shown center, with Muniz, left, and referee Octavio Meyran]. My friend Rose [wife of manager Vic Weiss], sitting next to me, had to give me a Valium—with beer." In 1984, Muniz encountered Napoles at a boxing tribute luncheon in East Los Angeles. As Muniz prepared to introduce his longtime ring rival, he recalled, "We were waiting around in the kitchen, when Napoles suddenly confessed, 'Armando, I want you to know, I was not responsible for what happened in Acapulco.'"

Frankie Duarte's bout versus Tarcisio "Famosito" Gomez (younger brother of featherweight Octavio "Famoso" Gomez) caused a memorable disturbance at the Olympic Auditorium on April 24, 1975. Duarte spoke to writer Dan Hanley: "Danny Lopez had just knocked out 'Chucho' Castillo in the bout before I came on, and the Mexican audience was none too pleased. Then, I win a very close decision over Gomez, also of Mexico. Now, [manager] John Cabrera had been telling me to acknowledge my fans. I had a habit of winning and then just leaving the ring. Well, this time I raise my arms to the crowd and I get hit in the head with a bottle. Now I'm mad, and I really upset the crowd by giving them the old 'shove it' sign. Now, they start to riot. They're throwing things in the ring, they're setting fire to the seats." Duarte, who needed a police escort to his dressing room, stated, "It was so bad that KCOP-TV cancelled their contract with the Olympic." Gomez (left) defeated Duarte (MD 10) in the rematch at the Olympic on May 29, 1975. (Courtesy of Frankie Duarte.)

Carlos Palomino's increasing confidence, ring intelligence, and powerful left hooks led to his stunning 1976 upset victory over WBC welterweight champion John H. Stracey (left) in London. Palomino's manager, Jackie McCoy, told the *Los Angeles Times*, "[Trainer] Noe [Cruz] and I felt very good about his chances. Carlos had looked very good in the gym. He kept hitting Stracey with body blows and kept breaking him. Carlos, more or less, walked through his punches." Stracey is shown saying goodbye to the belt as new champion Palomino salutes the Wembley Arena crowd.

Carlos Palomino (left) is pictured at a Friars Club banquet in Beverly Hills with actor Tony Danza (center) and comedian Milton Berle in 1981. Inspired by other athletes in television commercials, Palomino launched his show-business career by enrolling in an acting class at UCLA and soon landed a part on Danza's television series *Taxi*. Palomino appeared in movies such as *Geronimo* and *Price of Glory* along with television shows including *Knight Rider*, *Hill Street Blues*, *NYPD Blue*, *Highway to Heaven*, and *The White Shadow*. (Courtesy of Carlos Palomino.)

Armando Muniz recalled his matchup against fast-rising welterweight and future boxing superstar "Sugar" Ray Leonard (16–0) at the Springfield Civic Center in Massachusetts on December 9, 1978: "I needed the money and the only guy I could get a fight with was Leonard. I was in shape, but in retrospect, I was fighting time." In the third round, after Muniz was hit in the left elbow, his tendonitis began to flare up. At the end of the sixth round, much to Muniz's chagrin, his manager, Vic Weiss, stopped the bout, resulting in a TKO victory for Leonard. Muniz, who was paid a career high of $40,000, retired after the bout, stating, "I could have finished with one hand, but I didn't want to go out that way." By utilizing his positive image, commercial appeal, and popularity within the Mexican American community, Muniz (shown in 1980) became a pitchman for Schlitz Beer, travelling throughout the Southwest touting the slogan "*¡Tome el Gusto!*" ("Drink the Pleasure!").

Joey Olivo joined the professional ranks of boxing before graduating from Pueblo De Los Angeles High School (located in the Happy Valley barrio of Lincoln Heights) in 1978. Olivo, from the Ramona Gardens Housing Projects and the first American-born boxer to win the light flyweight title, told Jack Hawn in *Boxing Today*, "I was born and raised in Boyle Heights. I was a street fighter. That's how I got interested in boxing. Fights would just come my way, and I wouldn't walk away. I never lost a street fight. Actually, I had to fight to survive." Olivo, dressed in resplendent 1940s Pachuco clothing popular in Chicano culture, told Richard Hoffer of the *Los Angeles Times*, "I was in a gang growing up. Big Hazard was the name of the gang. We didn't wear colors; we just had the cholo-image, Pendleton shirts, pleated pants, Stacy Adams shoes, and derby hats." Olivo, pictured near Los Angeles City Hall in 1978, shopped for his clothes at a downtown pawn shop located near Seventh and Los Angeles Streets. (Courtesy of *Ring Mundial*.)

In 1978, *Entre Cuerdas* (a Los Angeles–based Spanish-language boxing magazine) honored popular Mexican American fighters from the Los Angeles area at a dinner event held at Casa Margaritas (located at 9911 West Pico Boulevard in Los Angeles). Invited to the Mexican restaurant were, from left to right, boxers Armando Muniz, Enrique Bolanos, Alberto "Superfly" Sandoval, Carlos Palomino, and Latino publicist Luis Magana. Kneeling in front is *Entre Cuerdas* publisher Jose Antonio Vazquez De La Torre.

Greg Puente, the popular "house fighter" of the Irvine Marriott Hotel, won the vacant California super featherweight title against tough Francisco "Pancho" Segura of Coachella (SD 12) on November 25, 1986. Puente recalled, "I personally lived in Alhambra right across the street from Danny 'Little Red' Lopez where I met him in 1979, and talked him into making me a fighter. I was really honored to be Danny's first fighter!" Boxing professionally from 1985 to 1993, the crafty Puente retired with 9 wins (4 knockouts), 6 losses, and 4 draws.

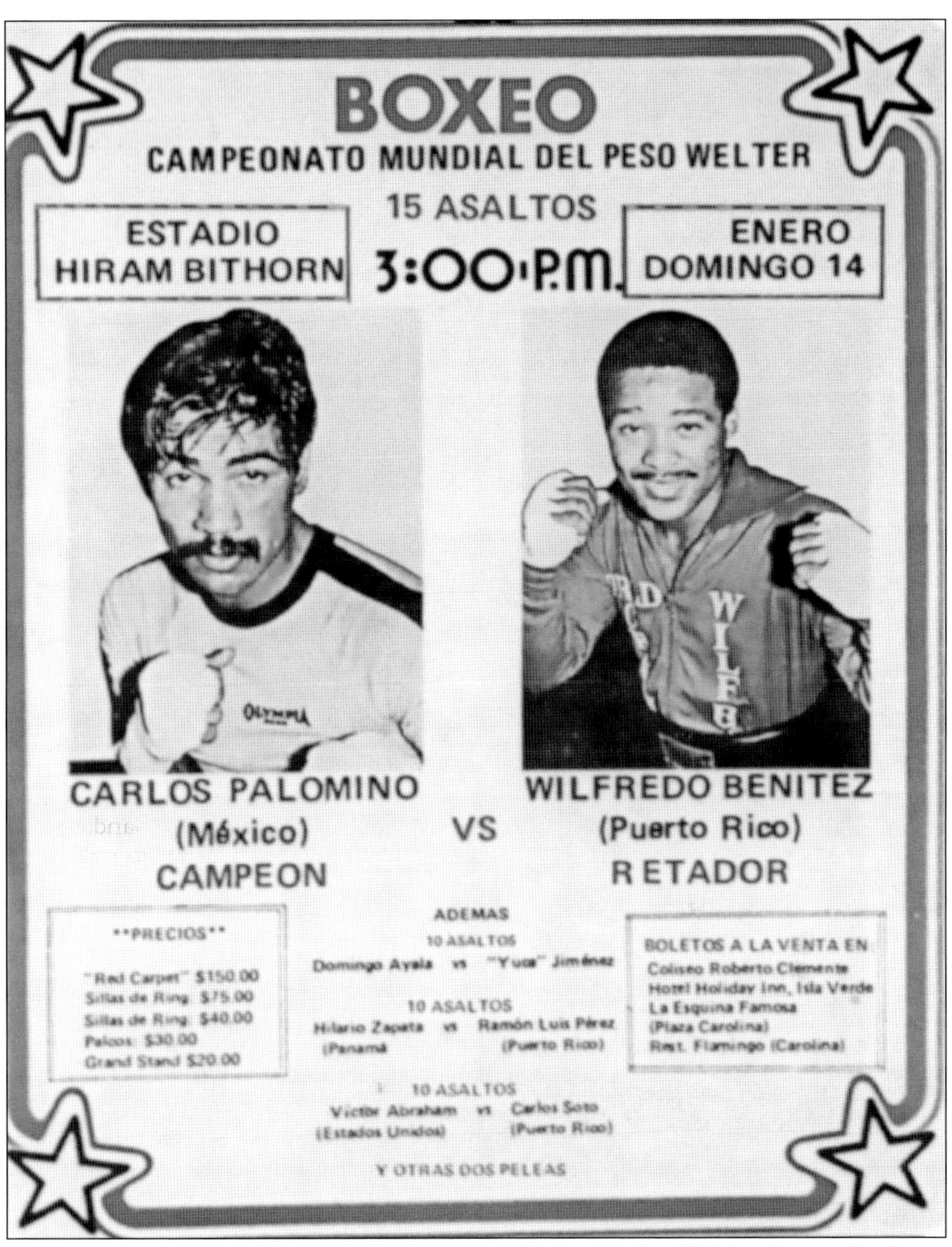

In another storied chapter of the Mexico–Puerto Rico boxing rivalry, WBC welterweight champion Carlos Palomino travelled to challenger Wilfred Benitez's backyard of San Juan, Puerto Rico, on January 14, 1979, to defend his title. Palomino recalled to *Uppercut* magazine, "We were told by the WBC that I had to go to Puerto Rico to defend my title. When I asked them why, I was told Benitez was the No. 1 contender, and the fight had to go to a purse bid. Puerto Rico came in with the highest bid, and my paycheck was $465,000 for the fight. I told them we would take half of that amount to put the fight in a neutral site. I even considered fighting him in New York, which was his second home. They said 'no,' and the WBC said if you don't go to Puerto Rico and fight, I would be stripped of the title. Back then, you did what you were told. Today, I would have gone to court and fought this."

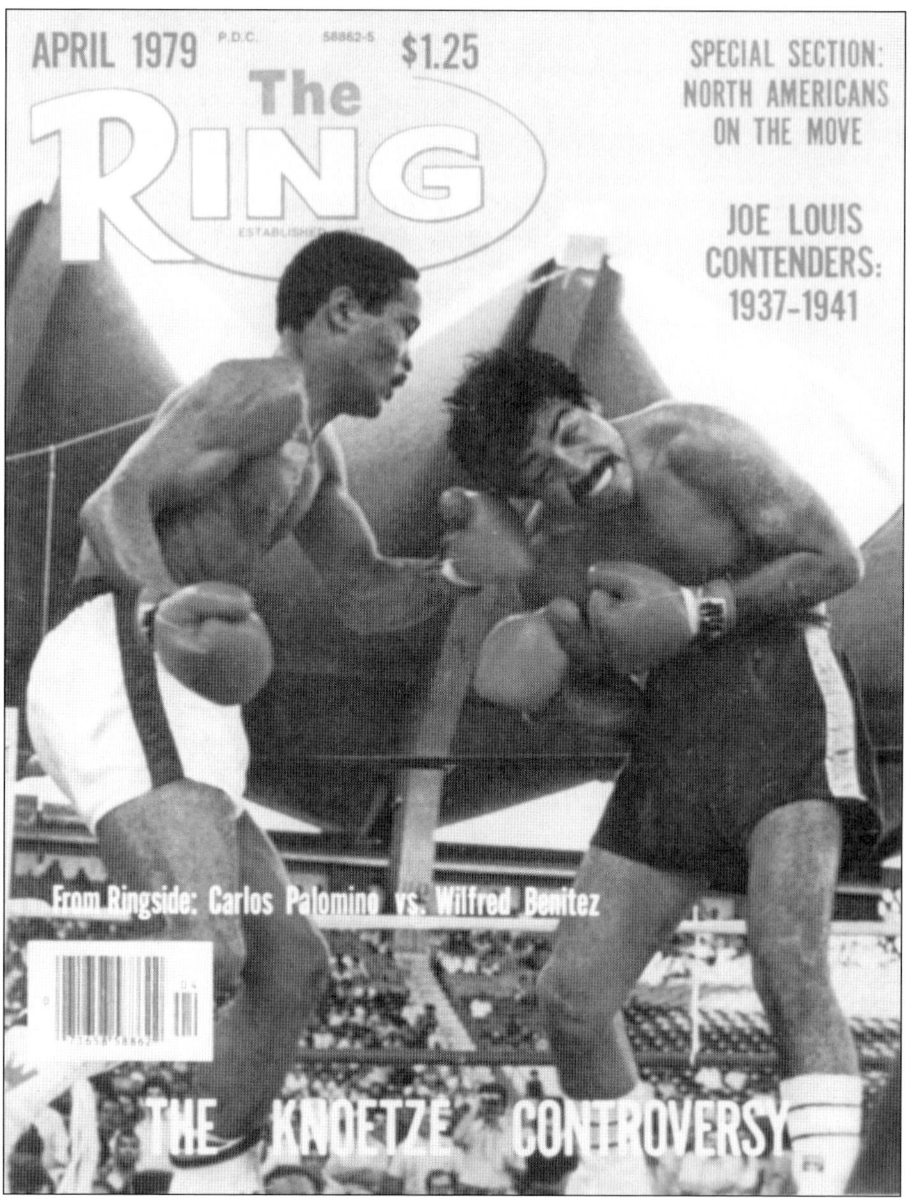

The *Los Angeles Times* reported on the negative factors affecting WBC welterweight champion Carlos Palomino's performance in the week before his fight against Wilfred Benitez in San Juan, Puerto Rico, on January 14, 1979: "Promoters threw open the doors to Palomino's San Juan gym, allowing Puerto Rican fans to swarm the Mexican-born boxer and disrupt his workouts." When Palomino (right) arrived at the site of his eighth defense against Benitez, he noticed how the boxing ring was set up on the baseball field at Hiram Bithorn Stadium. Palomino recalled, "The ring's in the middle of the field with a tarp over it. Half the ring's in the shade, half the ring's in the sun. He's in the shade, I'm in the sun." Palomino spoke of the arduous tropical Caribbean heat, "The dressing-room situation was criminal as far as I'm concerned. I was sitting there soaking wet, sweating from the humidity. No fan, nothing. When I went to Benitez's dressing room to congratulate him, that's when I learned about his air-conditioned locker room." (Courtesy of *Ring* magazine.)

Speaking more about his January 14, 1979, fight against Wilfred Benitez in Puerto Rico, Carlos Palomino concluded, "I also got taxed $60,000 from the Puerto Rican government. They told me it would count towards my taxes when I filed. Not true. They stole $60,000 from me. Bob Arum also promised me a rematch that I never got. I also found out that the WBC cancelled the automatic rematch clause for my fight with Benitez." Palomino said, "I absolutely thought I would have a tough time winning a decision against Wilfred in Puerto Rico and felt I needed a knockout to win the fight. He fought like he was the champion running around the entire fight and I had to chase him down. For me to get a split decision even on his home turf should tell fans I really won it." Palomino (right) told the *Los Angeles Times*, "I chased him for 15 rounds. He was elusive, but he just hit me pitty-pat punches. . . . I think I would have won any place else." Benitez was awarded the close victory and his second world title.

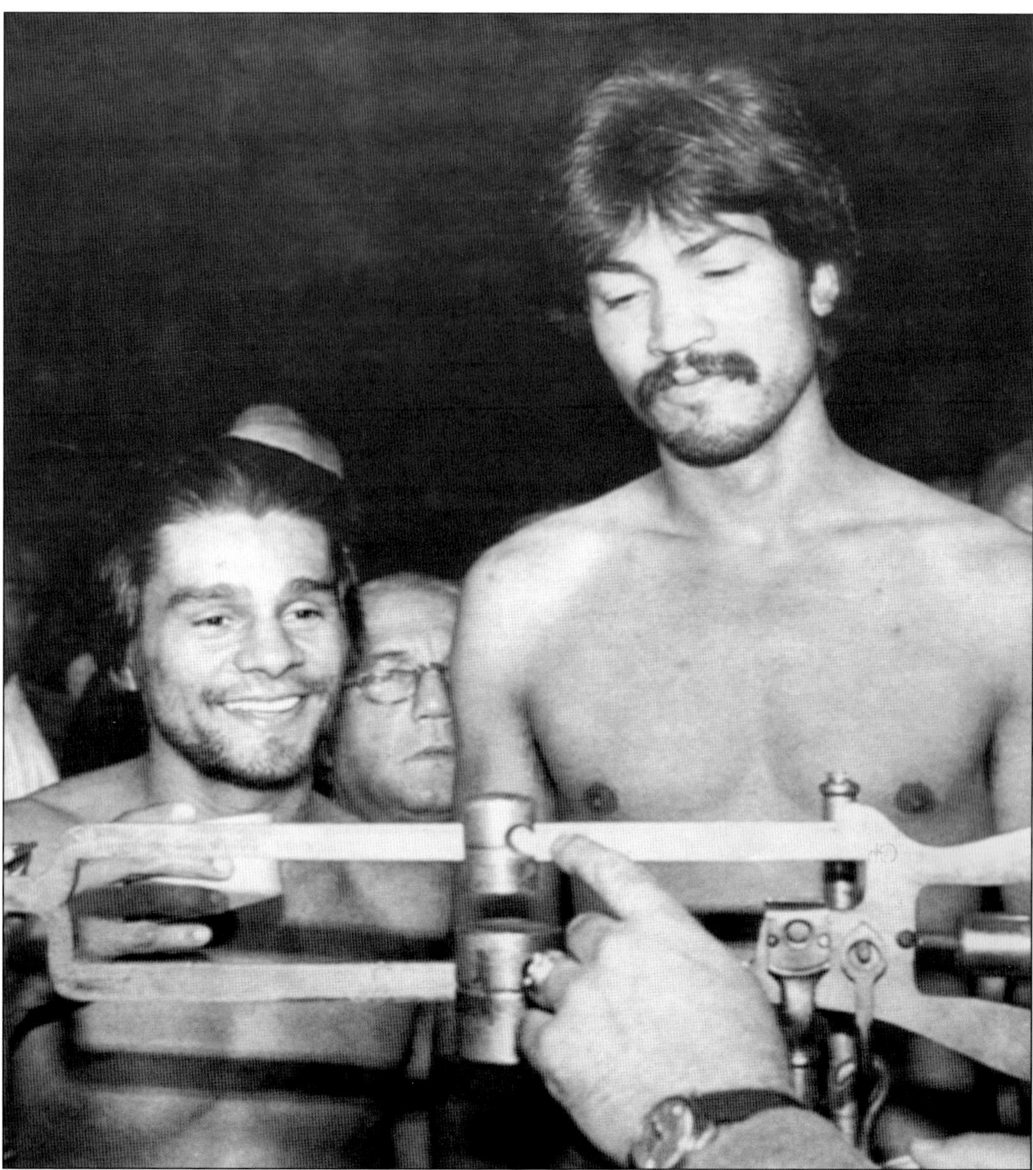

"King" Carlos Palomino (right), shown with "Manos de Piedra" ("Hands of Stone") Roberto Duran, weighs in for the "Dream Match" on June 22, 1979, at the venerable mecca of boxing, Madison Square Garden in New York City. In this battle of sizzling welterweights and former champions, Duran surprised Palomino with his quickness and feinting throughout the bout. Palomino, who was knocked down in the 6th round, lost a 10-round unanimous decision to Duran, telling Dan Hanley of cyberboxingzone.com, "The fight was originally scheduled for 12 rounds but was then cut to 10. I can't take anything away from Duran. He outhustled me with speed." Palomino recalled, "Before the bout, he comes up to me and shakes my hand. He tells me how much respect he has for me as a fighter. Then he asked me for an autograph for his son. To this day we hug when we see each other." The Palomino-Duran fight made the cover of *Sports Illustrated* and marked the beginning of a 17-year self-imposed ring retirement by Palomino.

Adrian Arreola, of Boyle Heights, discussed his close and hard-fought loss to future boxing monarch Julio Cesar Chavez at the Olympic Auditorium in 1983: "When I fought Chavez, it wasn't in my weight class, I had to go up to meet him. Chavez came right at me and I rocked him a few times. He was bigger than me, but I still gave him a tough fight." In 1984, the popular Arreola won the Stroh's Forum featherweight tournament (and $40,000 in prize money) by defeating Manuel Canela (KO 1). A year later, Arreola dropped a 10-round decision to future world champion Mario "Azabache" Martinez at the Sports Arena, saying, "Azabache was actually a much tougher fight for me than Chavez was. Because when I fought Chavez, I was younger, fresher, and more focused. But by the time of the Azabache fight, Al Stankie had me moving up and down in weight, plus Azabache was a good technician and boxer. It became just another fight. I was just looking for another paycheck." Adrian's brother Memo (left) and friend Jesse Ornelas (right) are shown celebrating with him on their shoulders in 1985. (Photograph by Carlos Baeza.)

Herman "Kid" Montes (right), shown with his younger brother John Montes at the Main St. Gym in 1979, retired from boxing in 1985 at the prime age of 26. Herman recalled, "After being a veteran boxer, the fights were far apart. Money was not frequent due to other boxers not wanting to fight me. I had a hard KO punch, and they knew it. I fought my idol, Pipino Cuevas, and it was something else to experience getting in that ring against an opponent you idolize as a fighter and I was able to knock him out in three rounds. Being the underdog, I then KO'd Francisco Lisboa eight months later in Indonesia. I got married right when I got back from Indonesia, now I am a husband training daily at the Main St. Gym in L.A., staying in shape waiting for the phone to ring. Six months go by and no world title offer. Boxing is very political, I was in love and I listened, so I quit boxing. Boxing was my life . . . I was depressed leaving my passion behind." (Courtesy of Herman Montes.)

Hector "El Torero" ("The Bullfighter") Lopez was born in Mexico City but raised in Glendale, California, since the age of three. Lopez, one of the world's top featherweights known for his thrilling fights, came up short in three world-title bids but defeated Georgie Navarro to take the $100,000 Stroh's Forum featherweight tournament in 1987. Forum fan favorite Lopez revealed, "I'm far from a choir boy. I may have [messed] up outside the ring, but inside the ring, I'm smart." Lopez's signature victory came over former world champion Juan Laporte (UD 10) at the Riviera Hotel & Casino in Las Vegas on May 8, 1992. Boxer/brawler Lopez captured the WBA Inter-Continental lightweight (1989), NABF super lightweight (1992), and WBO NABO super lightweight (1996) titles while managed by Johnny Flores and Harry Kazandjian (1990–1998) and trained by Gordon Wheeler. Lopez fought from 1985 to 2000, retiring with a record of 41 wins (23 knockouts), 7 losses, and 1 draw. Lopez (right) is shown in 1997 on his way to a victory (UD 10) over Israel Cardona in Kansas City. (Photograph by Bob Carson.)

Following Hector Lopez's knockout victory over Oscar "Negro" Bejines at the Los Angeles Sports Arena in 1988, talk soon began of a title shot, but a 28-month prison stint derailed those hopes. *Los Angeles Times* reporter Earl Gustkey wrote, "On October 9, Lopez's trademark, the locomotive-sized heart that had propelled him to a 17–1 pro boxing record, jumped the tracks. After a days-long argument with his girlfriend [Norma A. Gomez], Lopez, 21, surrendered to Glendale police, who arrested him on suspicion of kidnapping her at gunpoint." Lopez spoke to writer Ivan Goldman of the first-degree gun charges and beating his girlfriend's father and a family guest: "They got me for assault with bodily harm and assault with a deadly weapon. Actually, those are some of the nice things I did in those days." Lopez (center) is shown with ESPN boxing commentator Al Bernstein (left) and trainer Dub Huntley in 1997. The heavily tattooed Lopez, 44, passed away in Mexico City, his birthplace, from a drug overdose on October 24, 2011. Lopez's manager Harry Kazandjian said, "He was his own worst enemy. This kid had all the boxing skills in the world that anybody could dream." (Photograph by Bob Carson.)

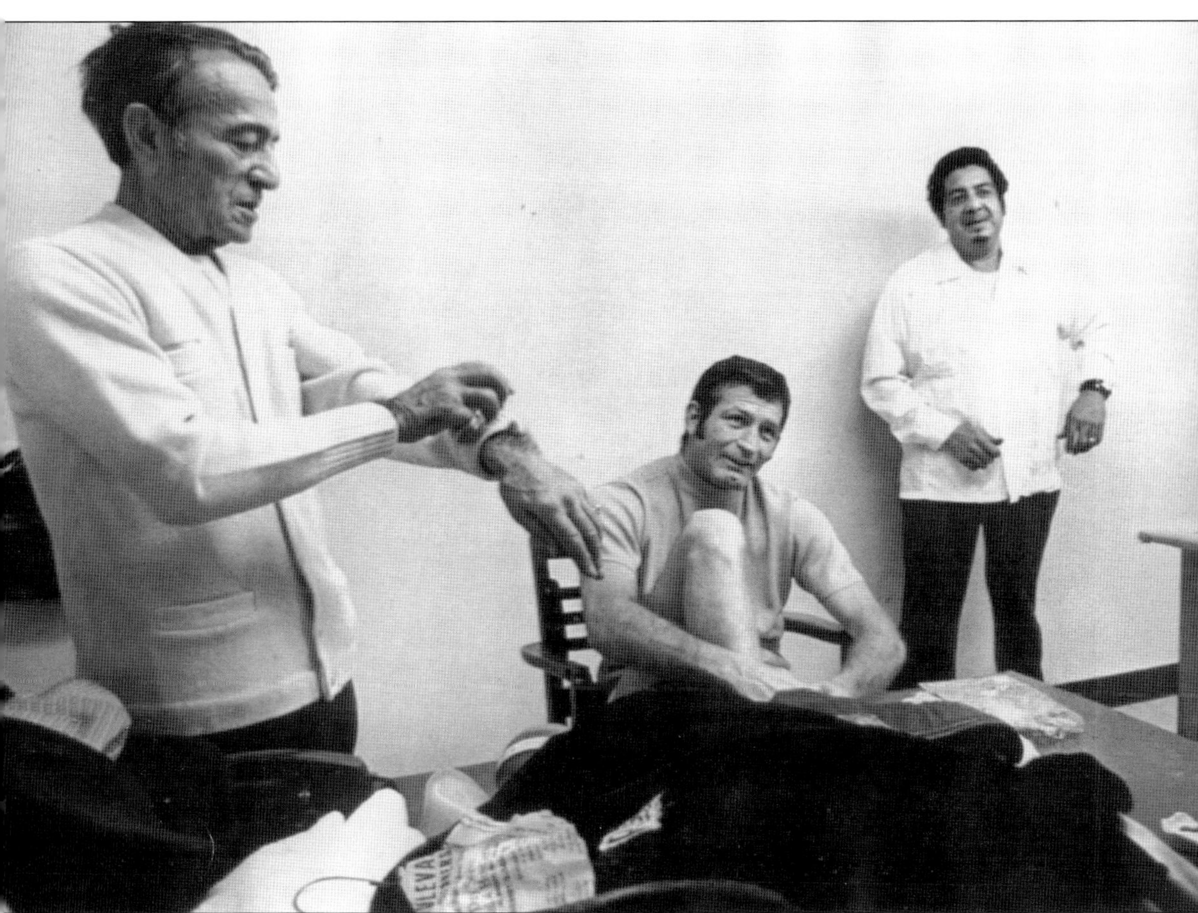

After Ernie "Indian Red" Lopez's last fight in 1974, the former contender toiled for 13 years as a truck driver, but in 1987, while casually attending a boxing show in Memphis, Tennessee, Lopez was—incredibly—talked into making a one-time, on-the-spot boxing comeback by friend/boxer Jimmy Heair and promoter Red Fortner. This ill-advised return to the ring resulted in Lopez, 41, being knocked out in the first round by welterweight newcomer Kenny Louis (7–2) at the Omni New Daisy Theater. Five years later, in 1992, Lopez vanished; he remained "missing" from family and friends until 2004, when he was located by Los Angeles Police Department detective Christine Beltran in a homeless shelter in Fort Worth, Texas. Lopez's return culminated in a CNN interview and celebratory induction into the California Boxing Hall of Fame that was held at Steven's Steakhouse in Commerce in 2004. Lopez (center), shown with manager Howie Steindler (left) and trainer Memo Soto, passed away at the age of 64 due to complications from dementia at Pleasant Grove, Utah, on October 3, 2009. (Photograph by George Rodriguez.)

The "Real" Paul Banke was a pressure-fighting southpaw born in Blythe, California, to parents Fred Banke (of Spanish Basque lineage) and Yolanda Miranda (of Mexican and Native American Yaqui blood). Yolanda stated in Banke's biography, *Staying Positive*: "Once he'd visited his first boxing club, that's where it took off. Paul had his calling." Banke began his professional career in 1985 and soon became a fan favorite at the Forum (fighting there a total of 12 times) under owner/promoter Dr. Jerry Buss. Banke captured the Stroh's Forum $100,000 super bantamweight tournament on September 13, 1988, with an exciting 11th-round TKO over Carlos Romero of Venezuela. Forum publicist John Beyrooty complimented the young fighter's stay-busy technique, stating, "Banke throws flurries from all angles," with journalist Ivan Goldman adding, "In a boxing match, sometimes a fight breaks out, and when Paul Banke was in the ring, a fight would always break out. He came to fight." Banke (right) is shown with trainer/former boxer Howard Mena of Houston, Texas, at a Great Western Forum Fight Night in 1990. (Photograph by Howard Mena.)

The "Real" Paul Banke (left), fighting out of Quail Valley, California, will forever be defined by his trilogy with Mexican warrior and perennial bleeder Daniel Zaragoza. In their second fight, on April 23, 1990, Banke won the title from WBC super bantamweight champion Zaragoza (TKO 9) in a brutal and punishing bout at the Great Western Forum. John J. Raspanti, writing for the West Coast Boxing Hall of Fame, stated, "The fight was a war from the opening bell. Banke stalked and popped. The Forum crowd screaming themselves hoarse as the two fighters went at it like rabid dogs. The ring was bloody by round nine when Banke teed up a left that put Zaragoza on his back. The champion beat the count and fought back bravely, but a perfect left hook crumpled him. Paul Banke was a world champion." Sportscaster Chick Hearn added, "Banke's hitting with everything but the ring post." Raspanti concluded, "Banke retired in 1993 at 29 with a record of 21 wins in 30 fights, with 11 knockouts. His hard-partying life had caught up to him. The drugs were eating him up."

The ring style of Paul Banke was to come forward, throw bombs, and bang away. In Banke's book, *Staying Positive*, former featherweight contender Ruben Castillo stated that Banke had "a heart bigger than his body. . . . They don't make fighters like that anymore." Banke, who grew up in Azusa, California, explained the feeling of winning the title to former champion Ray "Boom Boom" Mancini, "I became WBC world champion. No one can ever take that away from me. I'm in the history books. I love that." The *Los Angeles Times* called him "a champion with a reputation for wild fights and wild living," but the unfortunate lure of the street and temptations made available to the popular Banke proved to be overwhelming. On August 21, 1995, nearly two years after his last fight, Banke became the first major US boxer to publicly announce he had contracted the AIDS virus. In this image, Banke (center) stands with trainer Steve Rosenzweig (left) and ring announcer Jimmy Lennon Jr. moments after winning the world title in 1990. (Courtesy of Jimmy Lennon Jr.)

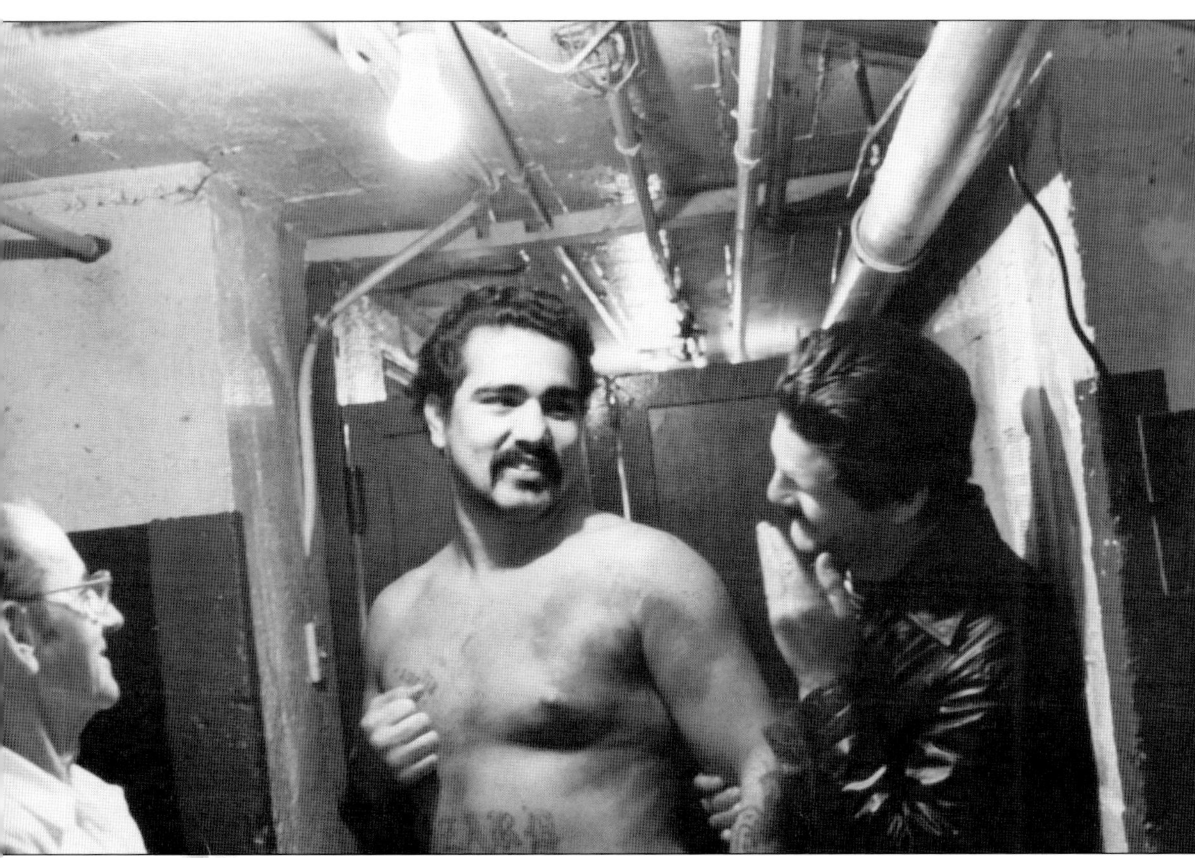

A boxing magazine once described heavyweight contender Eddie "The Animal" Lopez as having "more graffiti on his body than a New York subway." Known for his grittiness, Lopez told the *Los Angeles Times*, "You guys think it hurts getting stabbed with a knife? Try getting stabbed with a screwdriver." Lopez also reminisced about his childhood days, "In East L.A., you learn to fight before you learn to cry." Top-rated featherweight Ruben Castillo recalled to *Ring* magazine, "He came right at you, he would try to take your head off. That's all that mattered to him." WBC Continental Americas champion John Montes said, "He had a habit of hanging out with the wrong crowd. . . . No one could tell him what to do. He was that type of person." Lopez told la1news.com, "I was number five in the world, but I was always worried about making my next house payment." From left to right are gloveman Norm Lockwood, Lopez, and California Golden Gloves middleweight champion John Liechty in the catacombs of the Olympic Auditorium. (Photograph by John Liechty.)

Los Angeles Daily News sports columnist Mark Whicker wrote this about Eddie "The Animal" Lopez (left, shown with Gene Aguilera at the Main St. Gym): "On his stomach was a prominent 'Hazard' tattoo, signifying Big Hazard, the long-standing gang in East L.A. The rest of his torso was as much ink as skin. One night, Lopez knocked out Earl McLeay in 2:36 of the first round at the Silver Slipper in Las Vegas. 'Good job, Eddie,' called out Pat Cooper, the comedian. 'But I wasn't finished reading your back.' He was also a giant in his neighborhood, which hoped he'd become the first heavyweight champion of Mexican descent. The day before he fought [Gerry] Cooney, Lopez weighed in. Then he asked New York boxing writer Michael Marley what he was doing the rest of the day. 'Probably going to South Beach and drinking,' Marley said. 'I'm coming with you,' Lopez said. After a few hours of that, Marley reminded Lopez that he had an appointment the next day against a bad left hook. 'Shouldn't you be going back to the hotel?' Marley said. 'Nah,' Lopez said. 'Why change the routine now?'"

In the article, "Remembering Eddie Lopez, the Animal Who Laughed," sportswriter Mark Whicker wrote: "In 1980, Lopez got the call to fight Leon Spinks in eight days. . . . A few days after he got the draw with Spinks, Lopez got into a fight in the streets, where he was unbeaten one-on-one. Police officers came to the scene, and Lopez scored several knockouts before he was outnumbered, booked, and jailed. He told someone he could handle 5 cops, but not 12." Trainer/former boxer Rudy "Chicano" Hernandez told the *Los Angeles Daily News*, "I'm not going to tell you anything Eddie wouldn't have told you. When you get that PCP in you, you're going to fight, and it doesn't matter where. You couldn't keep Eddie away from it." Lopez (right), standing with amateur boxing champion John Liechty outside the Olympic Auditorium, sadly passed away at age 63 on July 14, 2017. His daughter Gloria "Glo" Rangel—one of 13 children Lopez fathered with five different women—said, "My dad didn't hide the fact that he enjoyed getting high. He would say he's a professional at it. Cause of death was an accidental overdose." (Photograph by John Liechty.)

Mia "The Knockout" St. John, born in San Francisco, traces the roots of her family name, Rosales, all the way to Zacatecas, Mexico. At the age of 29, St. John began her ring career and soon became one of the era's most popular female boxing champions. Working with the two most notable promoters in boxing (Don King and Bob Arum) allowed Mia to fight throughout the world while gaining valuable television coverage. St. John graduated from California State University, Northridge, with a degree in psychology and became the first boxer to appear on the cover of *Playboy* magazine (in November 1999). Eight years and 48 fights after her professional debut, St. John won her first world championship, the International Female Boxers Association world lightweight title (2005), followed by the WBC International Female welterweight (2008), WBC International Female lightweight (2008), and WBC World Female super welterweight (2012) titles. The lovely and talented St. John retired with a final tally of 49 wins (19 knockouts), 14 losses, and 2 draws earned while fighting from 1997 to 2016.

Don Chargin, the premier West Coast matchmaker of his era, worked over 3,000 bouts, promoting his first fight—at age 23—on Labor Day 1951 in his hometown of Santa Clara between former bantamweight champion Manuel Ortiz and local Eddie Chavez. In 1964, promoter Aileen Eaton hired Chargin away from the Bay Area so he could begin working at the Olympic Auditorium. A boxing scribe stated, "Los Angeles glitters with exceptional boxing talent and Chargin is the first to admit that he's fortunate in tapping the vast Mexican American fistic pool. 'I love for underdogs to win,' remarked Don. 'We've had a lot of shortenders win at the Olympic and that's good for our reputation. It shows people we're not putting in set-ups.'" After the retirement of Eaton and the arrival of new owner Jack Needleman, Chargin left the Olympic in 1984. After promoting fights in Northern California during the 1980s and 1990s, Chargin ("The Last Gentleman in Boxing") became senior advisor to Golden Boy Promotions from 2002 until his death in 2018. Standing from left to right are sportswriter Allan Malamud, manager Jackie McCoy, publicist Bill Caplan, and manager Howie Steindler; Chargin is seated in the chair at his home in Bell Canyon around 1975. (Photograph by Don Chargin.)

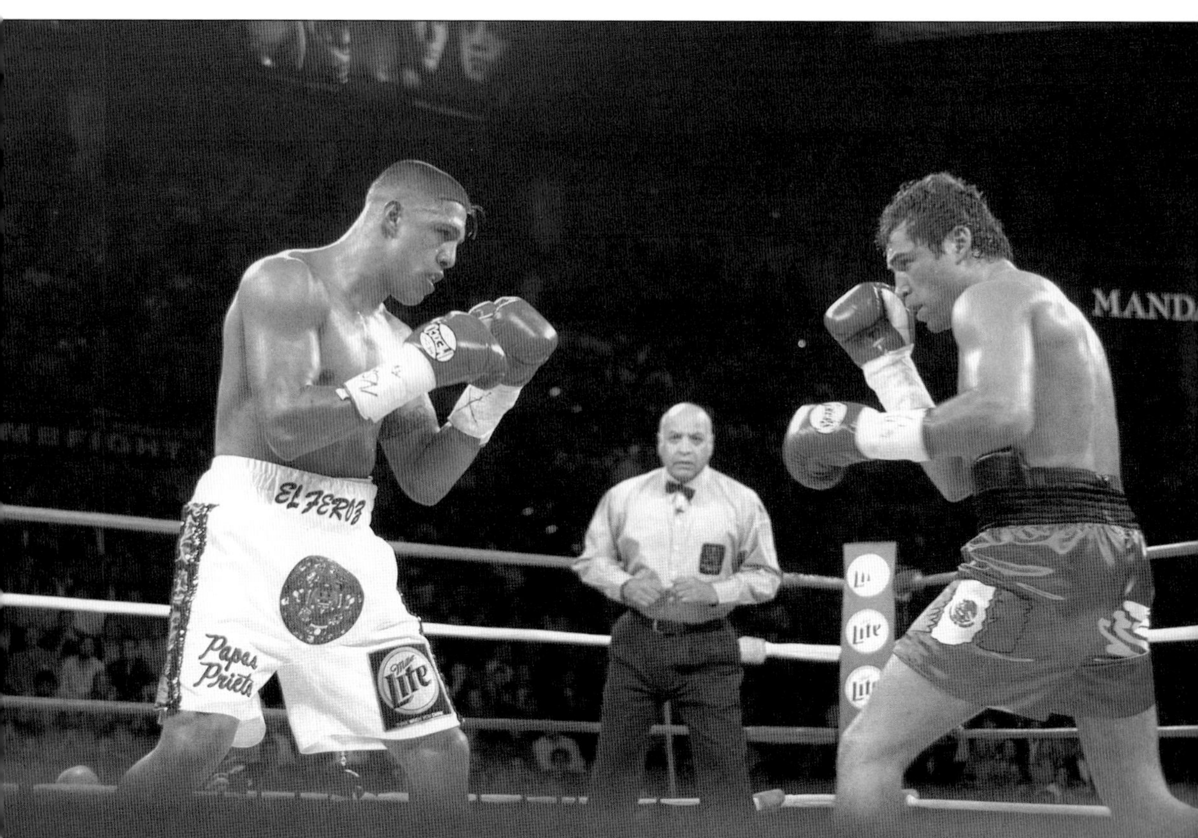

The buildup to the Oscar De La Hoya (right) vs. Fernando Vargas (left; referee Joe Cortez is between the opponents) mega-fight in 2002 was filled with piercing prefight slurs. The animosity began years earlier at a Big Bear training camp, when Vargas slipped and fell in a snowbank while doing roadwork. *Boxing News* wrote, "Vargas spotted De La Hoya chugging up the icy trail. Vargas said he held his hand out for a lift, but 'The Golden Boy' laughed and steamed past." During the hype, De La Hoya said, "Fernando Vargas is like a bull without a brain. But I'm like a bullfighter and I'm going to go for the kill." Vargas chimed in, "I hope I'm not chasing, and chasing, and chasing. Let me put it like this, we're gonna get down." At conclusion of De La Hoya's spectacular knockout victory over Vargas (TKO 11) in Las Vegas, Vargas left the ring without congratulating his adversary and skipped the customary post-fight interview with HBO. After a few days, De La Hoya and Vargas met privately at Smitty's Grill in Pasadena to settle their differences. De La Hoya later told his friend Javier Ruiz, "I've never been hit so hard in my life." (Photograph by Carlos Baeza.)

"Mighty Mike" Anchondo began his career under the tutelage of former WBA light flyweight champion Joey Olivo and his grandfather Fred Anchondo, along with assistance from bankers Jim Berklas and Gene Aguilera. Anchondo, a graduate of Bishop Amat High School in La Puente, was trained by Manuel "Chato" Robles when he took the WBC Youth World super featherweight belt in 2003. Anchondo was undefeated (24–0, with 18 knockouts) when he won the WBO super featherweight title (UD 12) in a thrilling battle over Julio Pablo Chacon of Argentina on July 15, 2004. Anchondo's taking of the WBO crown (vacated by Diego Corrales) was broadcast on HBO from the American Airlines Center in Dallas, Texas, and made him one of the first world champions under the banner of Golden Boy Promotions. The speedy Anchondo fought from 2000 to 2010, closing with a record of 30 wins (19 knockouts) and 3 losses, including triumphs over former world champions Gregorio Vargas, Mauricio Herrera, and durable contender Jose Luis Soto Karass. Anchondo is shown at the Oscar De La Hoya Youth Boxing Center (previously Resurrection Gym) at 1114 South Lorena Street in Los Angeles in 2003.

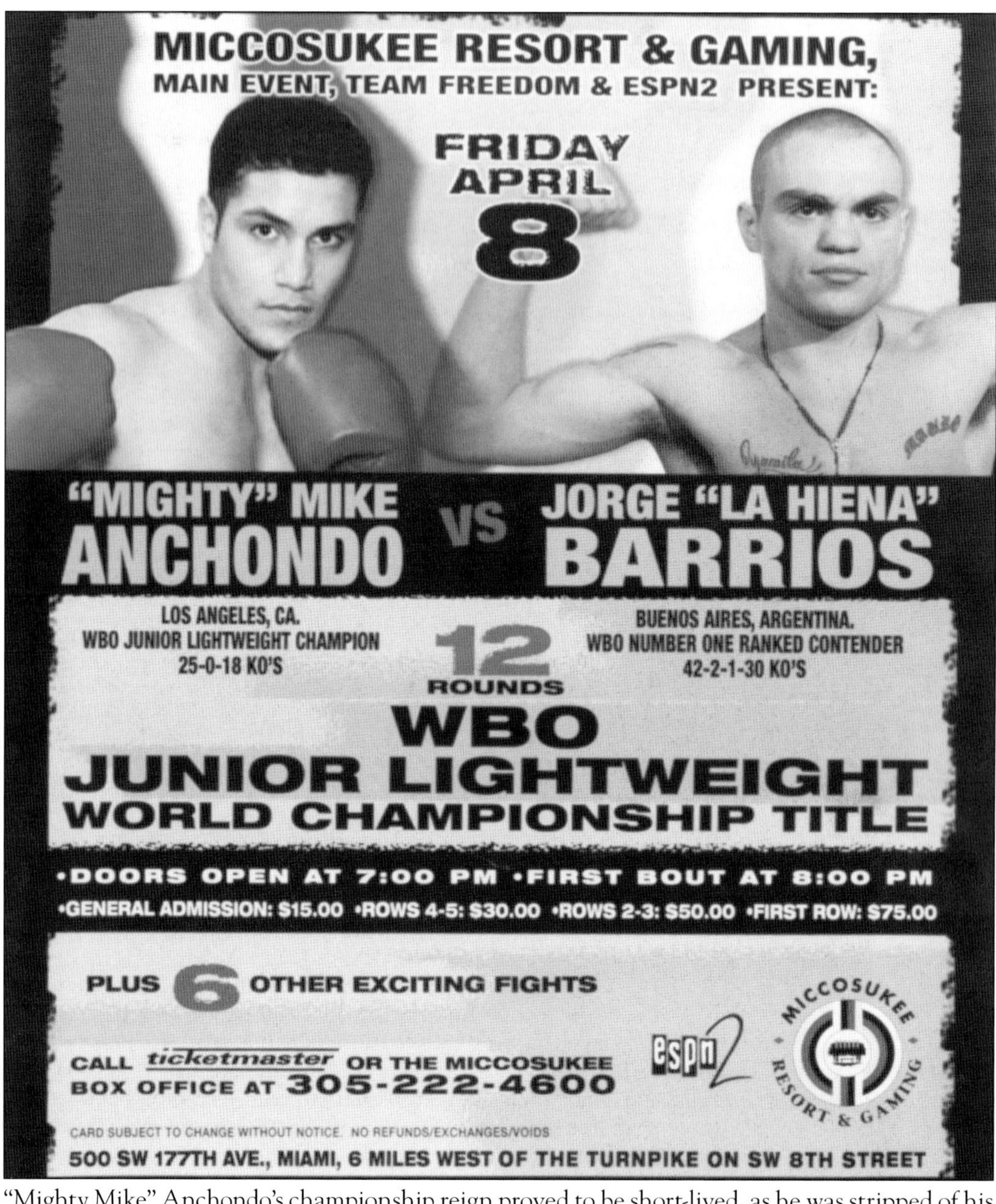

"Mighty Mike" Anchondo's championship reign proved to be short-lived, as he was stripped of his WBO super featherweight belt for being four and a half pounds overweight in his first title defense against Jorge "La Hiena" ("The Hyena") Barrios of Argentina. Anchondo recalled, "Training in Florida, in a mansion on Vero Beach, at 22, I felt like 'Wow, OK, this is how champions live.' Where I lacked discipline was outside of camp. I do not blame anyone for my bad decisions, only myself. I had to move my focus to dropping weight vs. focusing on my training and fight plan. I still showed up to the weigh-in completely dehydrated with a fever and felt weak. I was not about to give up and not fight. Fight night was a blur. Had I been even 50 percent of who I was that night, I could have easily beaten my opponent." Anchondo suffered a fourth-round TKO loss to Barrios in their title clash at Miccosukee Indian Gaming Resort in Miami, Florida, on April 8, 2005, in a bout televised by ESPN on *Friday Night Fights*.

In this image, "Mighty Mike" Anchondo (right) gets ready to unload a hard right on Mexico's Silverio Ortiz on his way to a fourth-round TKO victory at Santa Ana Stadium in 2003. Anchondo reflected, "After winning the world title, I signed a new contract with an East Coast promoter, which was not an easy transition. Being so young and only seeing the monetary aspect, I signed. I was unable to truly enjoy my well-deserved title, rather I worried about the business part of boxing that I had not been groomed for. I never once regretted winning that title that I worked my entire life for. I can now say after much mental and spiritual growth everything happens for a reason. The reality of it all, is that after a loss, people disappear and only the real ones stick around. Because from the rise and fall, I can say boxing is a family and I can tell you the true boxing fans never forget. So, the world title has always meant a lot to me and always will."

APPENDIX

WEIGHT CLASS DIVISIONS

Heavyweights	over 200 pounds
Cruiserweights	limit 200 pounds
Light Heavyweights	limit 175 pounds
Super Middleweights	limit 168 pounds
Middleweights	limit 160 pounds
Super Welterweights	limit 154 pounds (Junior Middleweights)
Welterweights	limit 147 pounds
Super Lightweights	limit 140 pounds (Junior Welterweights)
Lightweights	limit 135 pounds
Super Featherweights	limit 130 pounds (Junior Lightweights)
Featherweights	limit 126 pounds
Super Bantamweights	limit 122 pounds (Junior Featherweights)
Bantamweights	limit 118 pounds
Super Flyweights	limit 115 pounds (Junior Bantamweights)
Flyweights	limit 112 pounds
Light Flyweights	limit 108 pounds (Junior Flyweights)
Minimumweights	limit 105 pounds (Mini Flyweights, Strawweights)

SANCTIONING BODIES

NYSAC: New York State Athletic Commission (established in 1920)
NBA: National Boxing Association (established in 1921, changed to WBA in 1962)
WBA: World Boxing Association* (established in 1962)
WBC: World Boxing Council* (established in 1963)
NABF: North American Boxing Federation (established in 1969, affiliated with the WBC)
USBA: United States Boxing Association (established in 1976, affiliated with the IBF)
IBF: International Boxing Federation* (established in 1984)
WBO: World Boxing Organization* (established in 1988)
IBO: International Boxing Organization (established in 1988)
IBA: International Boxing Association (established in 1991)
IFBA: International Female Boxers Association (established in 1997)

*Major sanctioning bodies

Glossary

Disqualification (DQ): When the referee stops the bout due to an intentional, severe foul, the boxer breaking the rules or causing the injury shall lose by disqualification
Draw (D): When all three judges score the fight even, the bout is officially a draw, and no one is declared the winner
Knockout (KO): When a boxer is knocked down to the canvas by a legal punch and unable to rise up by the time of the referee's count of 10, he loses the bout
Majority Decision (MD): When two judges score the bout for the same boxer while the third judge scores it a draw
Majority Draw: When two judges score the bout a draw and the third judge scores for one of the boxers, the bout is called a majority draw, and no one is declared the winner
Split Decision (SD): When two judges score the bout in favor of one boxer while the third judge scores the fight for the other boxer
Split Draw: When one judge scores the bout for one boxer, the second judge scores for the other boxer, and the third judge scores it a draw, then no one is declared the winner
Technical Decision (TD): When a boxer is unable to continue due to an unintentional foul, accidental head-butt, injury, or cuts, and four rounds have been completed, the boxer ahead on the scorecards at the time is declared the winner
Technical Draw (also called **No Contest [NC]** or **No Decision [ND]**): When a bout ends prior to the completion of the fourth round due to an unintentional foul, accidental head-butt, injury, or cuts (or ends for reasons beyond the fighters' control), the fight is declared a technical draw, and no one is the winner
Technical Knockout (TKO): When a fighter is hurt by legal punches or cuts and can no longer continue as decided by the referee, the bout is stopped and awarded to the other fighter
Unanimous Decision (UD): When all three judges agree in scoring the bout for one boxer, that boxer is declared the winner of the fight

Bibliography

Banke, Paul, and Paul Zanon. *Staying Positive*. Sussex, UK: Pitch Publishing, 2019.
Boxing records. Retrieved 2018–2021. www.boxrec.com.
Dundee, Angelo. *I Only Talk Winning*. Chicago: Contemporary Books Inc., 1985.
Groves, Lee. *Tales from the Vault: A Celebration of 100 Boxing Closet Classics*. Charleston, SC: Lee Groves, 2010.
Maldonado, Marco A., and Ruben A. Zamora. *Pasión por los guantes: Historia del box mexicano 1, 1895–1960*. México, DF: Editorial Clio Libros y Videos, 1999.
Murray, Jim. *The Last of the Best*. Los Angeles: *Los Angeles Times*, 1998.
Seidman, Jay. *Latino Legends*. Lindenwold, NJ: Seidman Productions Inc., 2003.
Sugar, Bert Randolph. *Boxing's Greatest Fighters*. Guilford, CT: The Lyons Press, 2006.